IMMUNITY FOR MENTAL HEALTH

A COMPREHENSIVE PRACTICAL GUIDE FOR EVERYONE

DR. NITNEM SINGH SODHI

Made with ♥ on the Notion Press Platform
www.notionpress.com

Dedicated to my loving father.

Contents

Preface *vii*

About The Author *ix*

Part One

1. Introduction 3
2. Mindfulness 12
3. Physical Exercise 26
4. Positive Self-programming 42
5. Journaling 56
6. Social Support 63
7. Breathing Exercises 80
8. Art Therapy 90
9. Time Management 96
10. Sleep 101
11. Muscle Relaxation Techniques 105
12. Self-care 110
13. Self-improvement 118

Part Two

14. Anxiety Disorders 129
15. Depressive Disorders 135
16. Trauma Related Disorders 140
17. Addictions 146
18. Positive Self-affirmations 151
19. Diet & Nutrition 157
20. Emdr Self-therapy 162

Conclusion 165

Preface

As a practicing psychologist and psychotherapist, I have had the opportunity to work with thousands of patients who have struggled with a wide range of mental health issues. I have seen firsthand the devastating impact that these disorders can have on individuals and their loved ones. However, I have also witnessed the incredible resilience and strength of those who are able to overcome these challenges and reclaim their lives. It is my belief that everyone has the capacity for healing and growth, and this book is a reflection of that belief. In the following pages, you will find a comprehensive guide to building an immune system for your mind. Drawing upon my years of experience and research in the field of psychology and neuroscience, I have developed a unique approach to coping with and managing mental health disorders. My aim is to empower readers with the knowledge and tools they need to navigate the complexities of mental health and find lasting healing. Through a combination of practical strategies and individual guidance, this book provides a roadmap for building resilience, fostering emotional well-being, and achieving lasting recovery. Whether you are struggling with anxiety, depression, addiction, or any other mental health issue, this book is for you. It is my hope that the insights and techniques within these pages will serve as a beacon of hope and healing for all those who seek to improve their mental health and lead fulfilling lives.

Dr. Nitnem Singh Sodhi

About The Author

Dr. Nitnem Singh Sodhi is a renowned psychologist and psychotherapist, based in Lucknow, (U.P., India), known for healing thousands of patients suffering from a wide variety of mental health problems. With a doctoral degree in psychology and neuroscience, Dr. Sodhi has worked with reputed healthcare organizations such as Apollo Clinic and currently serves in the Indian Air Force.

Through his clinical experience as a therapist, Dr. Sodhi has witnessed the suffering of individuals unable to access help for their mental health problems. This inspired him to share his knowledge and techniques with others through his book, "Immunity for Mental Health: A Comprehensive Practical Guide for Everyone." In this book, readers can expect to learn coping mechanisms to manage and heal all types of psychological problems, along with detailed individual guidance on common mental health issues.

Dr. Sodhi is recognized by the India Book of Records and Asia Book of Records as the world's youngest neuro-psychologist. His research work, "The Unimind Metamodel" and "The Unibrain Theory," have revolutionized the field of psychology and neuroscience, providing the world's first unified model/framework of mind and brain. Dr. Sodhi has also developed his own innovative systems of therapy for the treatment of mental health disorders and has been a speaker at TEDx.

With nearly all his patients completely healed from mental health problems within 3-4 psychotherapy sessions, without any medications, Dr. Sodhi's clinical practice is highly regarded in the field of mental health. His book is a must-read for anyone seeking to build an immune system for their mental health and to overcome any mental health challenges they may face.

Part One

Coping Mechanisms for Mental Health

CHAPTER ONE

Introduction

Mental health refers to a person's overall psychological well-being, including their emotional, cognitive, and behavioral functioning. It encompasses a wide range of factors that contribute to a person's ability to function effectively in daily life, cope with stress, form and maintain relationships, and experience positive emotions.

The 4 major aspects of mental health include:

1. Emotional regulation: This refers to a person's ability to manage and regulate their emotions in response to different situations. Individuals with good emotional regulation are able to express their emotions in healthy and adaptive ways, without becoming overwhelmed or excessively reactive.

2. Cognitive functioning: This refers to a person's ability to think, reason, and problem-solve effectively. This includes skills such as attention, memory, decision-making, and executive functioning.

3. Social functioning: This refers to a person's ability to form and maintain healthy relationships with others. This includes factors such as communication skills, social support, and the ability to resolve conflicts effectively.

4. Resilience: This refers to a person's ability to bounce back from adversity and cope effectively with stress and challenges. Resilient individuals are able to adapt to changing circumstances and maintain a positive outlook, even in the face of difficult situations.

Mental health is an important aspect of overall health and well-being, and can have a significant impact on a person's quality of life. It is influenced by a wide range of factors, including genetics, environment, life experiences, and lifestyle choices, and can be improved through a variety of interventions such as therapy, medication, and self-care practices. One of such interventions are coping mechanisms.

Coping mechanisms can be helpful for managing a wide range of mental health problems, including some of the most common ones. Here is an exhaustive list of some of the mental health problems in which coping mechanisms can be useful:

1. Depression and other mood disorders, such as bipolar disorder and seasonal affective disorder.
2. Anxiety disorders, such as generalized anxiety disorder, panic disorder, and social anxiety disorder.
3. Post-traumatic stress disorder (PTSD) and other trauma-related disorders.
4. Obsessive-compulsive disorder (OCD) and related disorders.
5. Eating disorders, such as anorexia nervosa, bulimia nervosa, and binge-eating disorder.
6. Substance abuse disorders, such as alcohol and drug addiction.
7. Attention-deficit/hyperactivity disorder (ADHD) and related disorders.
8. Borderline and other personality disorders.
9. Schizophrenia and other psychotic disorders.
10. Insomnia and other sleep disorders.
11. Stress-related disorders, such as adjustment disorder and acute stress disorder.
12. Chronic pain and other physical health problems that impact mental health.
13. Relationship issues, such as difficulties with communication, intimacy, and trust.
14. Work-related stress and burnout.

Coping mechanisms can help individuals manage these mental health problems by providing them with effective strategies to reduce stress, manage difficult emotions, and improve their overall well-being. For example, coping mechanisms such as mindfulness, meditation, and deep breathing can help individuals manage symptoms of anxiety and stress. Cognitive-behavioral therapy techniques, such as cognitive restructuring and behavioral activation, can be effective in treating mood disorders and other mental health issues. Additionally, coping mechanisms such as exercise, proper nutrition, and adequate sleep can help improve overall physical and mental health.

Coping mechanisms can be viewed as an immune system for mental health based on the similarities between the two. Coping mechanisms are tools or strategies that help individuals manage stress and adversity, which can contribute to better mental health outcomes. Just as the immune system helps the body resist and recover from infections and illnesses, coping mechanisms can help individuals resist and recover from the negative effects of stress, trauma, and other challenges that can impact mental health. Developing and practicing coping mechanisms can help individuals build their mental resilience and strengthen their ability to manage difficult situations. Coping mechanisms can function as an immune system for mental health by helping individuals build resilience and manage stress. Stress can have negative effects on mental health, such as causing anxiety, depression, and burnout. Coping mechanisms provide tools and strategies that individuals can use to prevent stress from becoming overwhelming and causing these negative outcomes. By building mental resilience through coping mechanisms, individuals can develop an inner strength that allows them to better manage stress and bounce back from difficult situations.

Just as the immune system can be weakened by factors such as poor nutrition, lack of sleep, and stress, the effectiveness of coping mechanisms may be compromised by factors such as chronic stress, trauma, and mental health disorders. In some cases, professional help and treatment may be necessary to address mental health problems, just as medical treatment may be necessary to support the body's immune system.

Coping mechanisms can be helpful in managing various challenges and stressors, and can have a positive impact on all the 4 major aspects of mental health as discussed above. Here's how:

1. Emotional regulation: Coping mechanisms can help individuals manage and regulate their emotions in a healthy way. Some examples of coping mechanisms that can promote emotional regulation include deep breathing, meditation, exercise, or engaging in creative activities such as art or music. These coping mechanisms can help to reduce stress and promote a sense of calm and relaxation, which can be beneficial for emotional regulation.

2. Cognitive functioning: Coping mechanisms can also help to improve cognitive functioning, such as memory, attention, and problem-solving abilities. For example, cognitive-behavioral techniques such as thought challenging and cognitive restructuring can help individuals reframe negative or irrational thoughts, which can lead to improved cognitive functioning. Mindfulness practices can also be helpful in promoting cognitive functioning by improving attention and concentration.

3. Social functioning: Coping mechanisms can also be helpful in improving social functioning, such as communication skills, social support, and relationships. Engaging in social support can be a particularly helpful coping mechanism, as it can provide individuals with a sense of connection and belonging. Coping mechanisms such as assertiveness training or conflict resolution can also be helpful in improving social functioning.

4. Resilience: Coping mechanisms can be particularly beneficial in promoting resilience, which refers to an individual's ability to bounce back from adversity. Engaging in coping mechanisms that promote stress reduction and emotional regulation, such as exercise, mindfulness, or creative activities, can help to improve resilience. Additionally, coping mechanisms that promote social

support, such as seeking out help from others or engaging in social activities, can also be helpful in promoting resilience.

Coping mechanisms are simply the strategies or behaviors that individuals use to manage stress, negative emotions, and challenging situations. The primary function of coping mechanisms is to help individuals adapt to stress and difficult circumstances, and to reduce the negative impact of stress on mental and physical health.

Coping mechanisms can be adaptive or maladaptive. Adaptive coping mechanisms are effective and helpful in reducing stress and promoting well-being, while maladaptive coping mechanisms are ineffective or even harmful. Examples of adaptive coping mechanisms include problem-solving, seeking social support, mindfulness, exercise, and engaging in enjoyable activities. Examples of maladaptive coping mechanisms include substance use, self-harm, avoidance, and denial.

Coping mechanisms are an important aspect of mental health and can be useful for individuals in managing stress and difficult circumstances. By developing and utilizing effective coping mechanisms, individuals can reduce the negative impact of stress and improve their overall well-being. They are essential for maintaining good mental health because they allow individuals to effectively manage stress and difficult emotions, which are a natural part of daily life. Coping mechanisms refer to the strategies and behaviors that individuals use to deal with challenging situations, emotions, and thoughts in a healthy and adaptive way. Some common coping mechanisms include seeking social support, engaging in physical activity, practicing mindfulness and relaxation techniques, and engaging in creative activities or hobbies.

The ability to effectively cope with stress and adversity is crucial for maintaining good mental health because it helps individuals to regulate their emotions, reduce negative thoughts and feelings, and maintain a sense of resilience in the face of challenges. Without effective coping mechanisms, individuals may be more prone to developing symptoms of anxiety, depression, and other mental health conditions, as well as engaging in maladaptive coping behaviors such as substance abuse or self-harm.

Moreover, developing and utilizing healthy coping mechanisms can promote a sense of self-efficacy and self-esteem, as individuals feel more in control of their emotions and able to manage the challenges they face. Coping mechanisms can also promote positive social connections and a sense of community, which are important factors in maintaining good mental health.

Overall, developing healthy coping mechanisms is an important aspect of maintaining good mental health, and can have a positive impact on many different areas of an individual's life. If you are struggling to cope with stress or challenging emotions, seeking support from a mental health professional can be a helpful first step in developing more effective coping strategies.

When a person does not know any effective coping mechanisms and lives a stressful common lifestyle, it can lead to negative consequences for their mental and physical health. Without effective coping mechanisms, individuals may experience high levels of stress, anxiety, and other negative emotions, which can have a wide range of negative effects on the body and mind.

Here are some potential consequences of not having effective coping mechanisms and living a stressful lifestyle:

1. Mental health problems: Living in a chronic state of stress without adequate coping mechanisms can lead to mental health problems such as anxiety, depression, and post-traumatic stress disorder (PTSD).

2. Physical health problems: High levels of stress without effective coping mechanisms can also lead to physical health problems such as headaches, high blood pressure, heart disease, and a weakened immune system.

3. Maladaptive behaviors: Without healthy coping mechanisms, individuals may be more prone to engaging in maladaptive behaviors such as substance abuse, overeating, or self-harm as a

way to cope with stress and negative emotions.

4. Relationship problems: Chronic stress without adequate coping mechanisms can lead to relationship problems, as individuals may become more irritable, withdrawn, or less able to effectively communicate with others.

5. Reduced quality of life: Overall, living a stressful life without adequate coping mechanisms can significantly reduce a person's quality of life, leading to decreased enjoyment of activities, lower productivity, and a sense of hopelessness or despair.

It's important for individuals who are struggling with stress and negative emotions to seek out support and learn healthy coping mechanisms. This may involve seeking support from a mental health professional, practicing stress-reducing techniques such as mindfulness or exercise, or finding healthy ways to express emotions such as through creative activities or talking to supportive friends and family. The importance of having coping mechanisms that function as an immune system for mental health cannot be overstated. By providing tools and strategies for managing stress, coping mechanisms can help individuals build resilience, manage trauma and adversity, and maintain overall mental well-being. In this way, coping mechanisms can help protect mental health in the same way that the immune system protects the body from illness and disease.

Coping mechanisms are an essential tool for maintaining good mental health. They allow individuals to develop resilience and manage stress, anxiety, and other mental health issues effectively. This book offers readers a practical guide to coping mechanisms for mental health, which can be learned and practiced to build immunity against mental health problems. The coping mechanisms presented in this book work as an immune system for mental health. Just as the immune system protects the body from illness, these coping mechanisms protect the mind from the negative effects of stress, anxiety, and other mental health issues. By learning and practicing these coping mechanisms, individuals can build resilience and maintain their mental health.

One of the primary benefits of coping mechanisms is that they are adaptable and flexible. There is no one-size-fits-all solution to mental health issues, and coping mechanisms can be tailored to fit the unique needs of each individual. For example, some individuals may find that practicing mindfulness or meditation helps them manage stress and anxiety, while others may benefit more from cognitive-behavioral therapy or other techniques. This book offers a variety of coping mechanisms for readers to explore, allowing them to find the strategies that work best for them.

The coping mechanisms presented in this book are evidence-based and have been shown to be effective in helping individuals manage mental health issues. By learning and practicing these coping mechanisms, individuals can build resilience and develop the skills they need to manage stress, anxiety, depression, and other mental health issues. This can result in improved overall well-being and a greater sense of control over one's mental health. In addition to providing practical coping mechanisms, this book also offers insights into the factors that contribute to mental health issues. This can help readers gain a better understanding of their mental health and the challenges they face. By understanding the root causes of mental health issues, individuals can develop coping mechanisms that are specifically tailored to their needs. This can help them build resilience and maintain their mental health over the long term.

In conclusion, this book offers readers a practical guide to coping mechanisms for mental health. These coping mechanisms work as an immune system for mental health, protecting the mind from the negative effects of stress, anxiety, and other mental health issues. By learning and practicing these coping mechanisms, individuals can build resilience and maintain their mental health. Whether you are struggling with a mental health issue or simply want to maintain good mental health, this book has something to offer. The coping mechanisms presented in this book are evidence-based, adaptable, and flexible, allowing individuals to tailor their coping strategies to fit their unique needs. By reading this book, individuals can gain a better understanding of their mental health and the challenges they face, and develop the skills they need to manage these challenges effectively.

CHAPTER TWO

Mindfulness

Mindfulness is a practice of intentionally paying attention to the present moment, without judgment. It involves becoming more aware of one's thoughts, feelings, and bodily sensations, as well as the environment around us. Mindfulness is often practiced through meditation, although it can also be incorporated into daily activities and routines.

The benefits of mindfulness practice are numerous, both for mental and physical health. Research has shown that regular mindfulness practice can help to reduce stress, anxiety, and depression, improve focus and attention, enhance emotional regulation, and improve overall well-being. In addition, mindfulness has been found to have a positive impact on physical health, with research suggesting that it can help to lower blood pressure, reduce chronic pain, and improve immune system function. Furthermore, mindfulness has been found to be a valuable tool for enhancing relationships, both with oneself and others. By cultivating non-judgmental awareness and compassion, individuals can improve their ability to communicate effectively and empathize with others. Additionally, practicing mindfulness can help individuals to become more aware of their own patterns of behavior and thought, which can lead to greater self-awareness and personal growth.

The practice of mindfulness can be particularly beneficial as a coping mechanism, especially when dealing with stress, anxiety, or difficult emotions. By focusing on the present moment and becoming more aware of our thoughts and feelings, mindfulness can help individuals to better manage their reactions to challenging situations. Instead of becoming overwhelmed by negative thoughts and emotions, individuals can learn to acknowledge them without judgment, and develop greater control over their response.

Research has shown that mindfulness can be effective in reducing symptoms of anxiety, depression, and other mental health challenges. By practicing mindfulness regularly, individuals can also develop greater resilience and improve their overall well-being. In addition, mindfulness has been found to have positive effects on physical health, such as reducing chronic pain and improving immune system function. Overall, mindfulness is a valuable coping mechanism that can help individuals to better manage their emotions, improve their mental and physical health, and develop greater resilience in the face of life's challenges.

Learning mindfulness can work as an immune system for mental health in several ways. Just as our physical immune system helps protect us from harmful bacteria and viruses, our mental immune system helps protect us from negative thoughts, emotions, and stressors that can harm our mental health. Mindfulness can strengthen our mental immune system by helping us to become more aware of our thoughts, emotions, and behaviors, and develop greater control over our responses to them. One way that mindfulness works as an immune system for mental health is by reducing stress and anxiety. Mindfulness involves intentionally focusing on the present moment, which can help to quiet the mind and reduce racing thoughts. By reducing stress and anxiety, mindfulness can help to protect against the negative effects of chronic stress, such as fatigue, depression, and burnout. Additionally, mindfulness can help to improve emotional regulation. By becoming more aware of our emotions and learning to observe them without judgment, we can develop greater control over our reactions to them. This can help us to better manage difficult emotions, such as anger or sadness, and protect against the negative effects of emotional dysregulation, such as impulsivity or irritability. Furthermore, mindfulness can also help to improve our overall well-being by promoting positive mental states such as happiness and contentment. Regular mindfulness practice has been linked to improved mood, increased self-esteem, and greater life satisfaction, which can help protect against the negative effects of mental health challenges such as depression and anxiety.

In summary, by developing greater awareness and control over our thoughts, emotions, and behaviors, mindfulness can act as an immune system for mental health. By reducing stress and anxiety, improving emotional regulation, and promoting positive mental states, mindfulness can help to protect against the negative effects of mental health challenges and improve overall well-being.

There are many different ways to practice mindfulness, and individuals may find different techniques or methods that work best for them. Some common mindfulness practices include:

1. **Mindful breathing** : Focusing on the sensation of breathing, and bringing attention back to the breath whenever the mind wanders.

Mindful breathing is a technique used in mindfulness meditation to cultivate present moment awareness and focus on the breath. It involves bringing attention to the sensations of the breath as it moves in and out of the body, and observing these sensations without judgment or distraction.

To practice mindful breathing, follow these steps:

1. Find a quiet space where you can sit comfortably and without distractions.

2. Close your eyes and take a few deep breaths to relax and settle into the present moment.

3. Begin to focus your attention on the sensation of the breath moving in and out of your body. You may choose to focus on the sensation of the breath at the nostrils, the rise and fall of the chest, or the sensation of the breath in the belly.

4. Notice the sensations of the breath without trying to control it or change it in any way. Simply observe the breath as it is.

5. As you focus on the breath, you may notice that your mind begins to wander. When this happens, gently bring your attention back to the breath, without judging yourself or the distraction.

6. Continue to focus on the breath for the duration of your practice, whether it is a few minutes or longer.

Mindful breathing can be done at any time, whether you're sitting in meditation or engaged in daily activities. You can take a few moments to focus on the breath when you're feeling stressed or overwhelmed, or incorporate mindful breathing into your regular routine. Remember, the goal of mindful breathing is not to force your mind to be quiet or to eliminate thoughts, but to bring your attention back to the present moment and cultivate a sense of calm and awareness. The philosophy behind the practice of mindful breathing is rooted in the principles of mindfulness, which is a type of meditation that focuses on developing awareness of the present moment. Mindfulness involves bringing a non-judgmental and curious attention to our thoughts, feelings, and bodily sensations as they arise, without getting caught up in them or reacting to them.

When we focus on our breath during mindful breathing, we're bringing our attention to the present moment and to the physical sensations of our breath moving in and out of our body. This can help us to cultivate a sense of calm and awareness, as well as to quiet the chatter of the mind. By paying attention to the breath in a non-judgmental way, we can learn to observe our thoughts and feelings without getting caught up in them. This can help us to develop greater clarity and perspective on our experiences, and to develop greater emotional regulation and resilience.

In addition, the practice of mindful breathing has been shown to have physical benefits, such as reducing stress and anxiety, lowering blood pressure, and improving overall well-being. It is a simple and accessible practice that can be done anytime, anywhere, making it a valuable tool for improving our mental and physical health.

2. **Body scan meditation** : Bringing attention to different parts of the body, and noticing sensations without judgment.

Body scan meditation is a mindfulness technique that involves systematically focusing your attention on each part of your body, from your toes to the top of your head. The purpose of this practice is to develop awareness of physical sensations and to release any tension or stress in the body.

Here's a step-by-step guide to practicing body scan meditation:

1. Find a quiet, comfortable space where you can lie down on your back without being disturbed.

2. Close your eyes and take a few deep breaths to relax and settle into the present moment.

3. Begin to focus your attention on the sensations in your toes. Notice any tension, discomfort, or warmth in this area. Don't try to change anything, simply observe the sensation.

4. Slowly move your attention up your body, paying attention to each area in turn, including your feet, legs, hips, stomach, chest, arms, hands, neck, and head. Spend a few moments focusing on each area, noticing any sensations or feelings that arise.

5. If you notice any tension or discomfort in a particular area, try to relax that part of your body as you continue to breathe deeply.

6. If your mind starts to wander or you become distracted, simply bring your attention back to the area of the body you were focusing on.

7. Once you've scanned your entire body, take a few deep breaths and slowly begin to wiggle your fingers and toes to come out of the meditation.

You can do a body scan meditation for as little or as long as you like. Some people prefer to start with a shorter practice, such as 5-10 minutes, and gradually increase the duration over time.

Body scan meditation can be a useful tool for reducing stress and anxiety, increasing relaxation, and improving sleep quality. It can also help you develop greater awareness of your body and improve your ability to focus on the present moment. In body scan meditation, we focus our attention on the physical sensations in our body, moving our attention from one area of the body to the next. The purpose of this practice is to develop awareness of physical sensations and to release any tension or stress in the body. By scanning the body in a systematic way, we learn to observe our physical sensations without getting caught up in them, and we become more aware of areas of tension or discomfort. This allows us to relax these areas and release physical stress, which can in turn help to reduce mental and emotional stress as well.

The practice of body scan meditation can also help us to cultivate greater self-awareness, as we become more attuned to the physical sensations in our body and the emotions that are associated with them. This increased awareness can help us to respond more effectively to stress and other challenges in our lives. Overall, the philosophy behind body scan meditation is to use the body as a gateway to the present moment and to develop greater awareness and non-judgmental observation of our physical sensations, thoughts, and emotions. This can help us to reduce stress, increase relaxation, and improve our overall well-being.

3. **Mindful movement** : Engaging in physical activity such as yoga or walking, while intentionally focusing on the present moment.

Mindful movement is a type of mindfulness practice that involves bringing awareness and attention to our physical movements and bodily sensations while engaging in physical activity, such as yoga or walking. The aim of this practice is to cultivate a greater sense of mindfulness and presence, and to deepen our connection with the body and the present moment.

To practice mindful movement, you can follow these steps:

1. Choose an activity: First, choose an activity that involves physical movement, such as yoga, walking, running, or swimming. It's best to choose an activity that you enjoy and that you can do regularly.

2. Focus on the breath: As you engage in the activity, bring your attention to your breath. Notice the sensation of the breath moving

in and out of your body, and try to synchronize your movements with your breath.

3. Observe bodily sensations: Notice the physical sensations in your body as you move. Pay attention to the way your muscles feel, the way your body moves through space, and any other sensations that arise.

4. Bring non-judgmental awareness: If you notice any thoughts or emotions arising, simply observe them without judgment or attachment. Notice them and let them pass, without getting caught up in them.

By practicing mindful movement, we can develop greater awareness of our physical movements and the sensations in our body. This can help us to cultivate a greater sense of mindfulness and presence, and to deepen our connection with the present moment. It can also help to reduce stress, increase relaxation, and improve our overall well-being. In addition, the practice of mindful movement has been shown to have physical benefits, such as reducing pain, improving posture and balance, and increasing flexibility and range of motion. It can be a valuable tool for improving both our mental and physical health.

4. **Mindful eating** : Bringing attention to the sensations of eating, such as the taste, texture, and smell of food.

Mindful eating is a type of mindfulness practice that involves paying close attention to the experience of eating, with an open and non-judgmental attitude. The aim of this practice is to deepen our connection with the food we eat, to become more aware of the sensations in our body, and to cultivate a greater sense of mindfulness and presence in our daily lives.

To practice mindful eating, you can follow these steps:

1. Slow down: Take the time to slow down and savor each bite of food, rather than rushing through your meal.

2. Engage your senses: Use your senses to engage with the food. Notice the color, texture, and aroma of the food, as well as the way

it feels in your mouth and the way it tastes.

3. Tune in to your body: Pay attention to the physical sensations in your body as you eat. Notice feelings of hunger, fullness, and satisfaction, as well as any other bodily sensations that arise.

4. Be present: Try to stay present and focused on the experience of eating, rather than getting distracted by other things.

Mindful eating has been shown to have a number of benefits, both physical and psychological. Some of the benefits of mindful eating include:

1. Improved digestion: By slowing down and savoring each bite, we can help our bodies to digest food more effectively.

2. Increased satisfaction: By paying closer attention to the sensations of hunger and fullness in our body, we can improve our satisfaction with meals and reduce overeating.

3. Reduced stress and anxiety: Mindful eating can help us to reduce stress and anxiety by increasing our sense of mindfulness and presence in the moment.

4. Improved relationship with food: By developing a more conscious and attentive relationship with food, we can develop a healthier relationship with food and our bodies.

Overall, the practice of mindful eating can be a valuable tool for improving our overall health and well-being. By becoming more aware of the sensations in our body and the experience of eating, we can deepen our connection with the present moment and cultivate a greater sense of mindfulness in our daily lives.

5. **Gratitude affirmations** : positive statements that express appreciation for the good things in one's life and can help cultivate a sense of gratitude and positivity.

Gratitude affirmations can bring a state of mindfulness by helping individuals focus on the present moment and cultivate an attitude of gratitude. Mindfulness is a state of awareness in which individuals focus on their present experiences and thoughts without judgment. Gratitude affirmations can be a useful tool for cultivating mindfulness because they encourage individuals to focus on positive experiences and thoughts, which can help to reduce stress and promote well-being. When individuals practice gratitude affirmations, they are actively seeking out positive experiences and focusing on the things they are grateful for. This can help to shift their mindset from one of negativity and stress to one of positivity and appreciation. By focusing on positive experiences and emotions, individuals can reduce stress and improve their mental well-being. Gratitude affirmations can also help individuals develop a greater sense of empathy and compassion, which can further enhance their mindfulness practice. In addition to promoting mindfulness, gratitude affirmations can also help individuals develop a greater sense of resilience and coping ability. By focusing on positive experiences and emotions, individuals can build a sense of gratitude that can help them cope with difficult situations and stressors. This sense of gratitude can also help individuals maintain a positive outlook and a sense of hope, which can be important for mental health and well-being.

Gratitude affirmations are positive statements that focus on feeling thankful and appreciative for the good things in your life. Affirmations can be used to cultivate a sense of gratitude and positivity, and can help shift your mindset towards a more optimistic and thankful perspective. There is scientific evidence to suggest that practicing gratitude can have a positive impact on mental health and well-being. For example, a study published in the Journal of Personality and Social Psychology found that people who wrote letters expressing gratitude experienced significant increases in happiness and life satisfaction, and decreases in symptoms of depression, compared to people who wrote about negative experiences or simply wrote about everyday events. Another study, published in the journal Applied Psychology: Health and Well-Being, found that people who engaged in a daily gratitude journaling practice for just two weeks experienced improvements in mood, optimism, and life satisfaction.

While there is still more research needed to fully understand the benefits of gratitude affirmations and other gratitude practices, these studies suggest that incorporating gratitude into your daily life can have a positive impact on your well-being.

Practicing gratitude affirmations is a powerful way to cultivate a positive mindset and increase overall well-being. Here are some tips for practicing gratitude affirmations:

1. Find a quiet and comfortable space where you feel relaxed and safe.

2. Start with small things you are grateful for, such as a delicious meal or a kind message from a friend.

3. Use words that resonate with you and feel authentic.

4. Visualize and feel the emotion behind the affirmations to make them more powerful.

5. Repeat the affirmations regularly, ideally daily, to create a habit of gratitude.

6. Focus on the present moment to help ground yourself and reduce stress.

By incorporating these tips into your gratitude practice, you can enhance your mood and overall well-being.

At its core, the philosophical mechanism underlying gratitude affirmations is the idea that by focusing on the positive aspects of our lives and expressing appreciation for them, we can cultivate a sense of gratitude and well-being.

Gratitude is a complex emotion that involves acknowledging and recognizing the good things in our lives, and feeling thankful and appreciative for them. By practicing gratitude affirmations, we can train our minds to focus on the positive aspects of our lives and shift our perspective towards a more optimistic and appreciative mindset. From a perspective, gratitude affirmations can be seen as a form of positive thinking or positive psychology. They are grounded in the idea that our thoughts and emotions have a powerful impact on our overall well-being, and that by intentionally cultivating positive thoughts and emotions, we can enhance our mood, increase resilience, and improve our quality of life. The practice of gratitude affirmations also aligns with many spiritual and religious traditions, which emphasize the importance of gratitude as a way to connect with a higher power or the universe. By expressing gratitude for the good things in our lives, we can cultivate a deeper sense of connection and purpose. Overall, the core philosophical mechanism underlying gratitude affirmations is the idea that by focusing on the positive and expressing gratitude, we can cultivate a sense of well-being, resilience, and connection in our lives.

Expressing gratitude towards God can be a wonderful way to focus your mind on positivity and to develop a deeper sense of connection and spirituality. The concept of gratitude affirmations directed towards God is to cultivate a sense of thankfulness and appreciation for the blessings in your life, as well as for the grace and guidance provided by a higher power or divine force. This practice can help you to develop a more positive mindset, improve your overall well-being, and deepen your sense of connection to something greater than yourself. The mechanisms of gratitude affirmations directed towards God involve intentionally focusing your attention on the things that you feel grateful for, and expressing your appreciation through words or thoughts directed towards the divine. This can help to shift your perspective towards the positive aspects of your life, and may also help you to feel more connected to your spirituality or sense of purpose. To practice gratitude affirmations directed towards God, you can use phrases such as "Thank you, God, for..." or "I am grateful for the blessings you have given me, such as...". You may choose to focus on specific areas of your life, such as your health, relationships, or work, or simply express gratitude for the many small joys and gifts that fill your days. It can be helpful to make this practice a regular part of your routine, such as by incorporating it into your daily meditation or prayer practice.

There is scientific evidence that practicing gratitude, including gratitude affirmations directed towards God, can have a positive impact on our mental and physical well-being. Research has shown that regularly practicing gratitude can increase positive emotions, reduce symptoms of depression, improve sleep quality, and increase feelings of social support and connection. One study published in the Journal of Positive Psychology found that writing gratitude letters to God or a higher power was associated with significant increases in happiness and life satisfaction among participants. Other studies have shown that gratitude can also have physical health benefits, such as reducing inflammation and improving cardiovascular health. For example, a study published in the journal Applied Psychology: Health and Well-being found that participants who practiced gratitude for eight weeks had lower levels of inflammation and improved heart rate variability compared to a control group. Overall, the evidence suggests that incorporating gratitude affirmations directed towards God or a higher power can be a powerful tool for improving mental and physical health, as well as cultivating a deeper sense of spirituality and connection.

Discussion

Mindfulness is a practice that involves intentionally bringing your attention to the present moment, without judgment or distraction. The beauty of mindfulness is that it can be practiced anywhere, anytime, and by anyone. Whether you're at home, at work, or on the go, you can cultivate mindfulness and reap its benefits.

One simple way to practice mindfulness is by paying attention to your breath. You can take a few deep breaths, noticing the sensation of air moving in and out of your body. If your mind wanders, gently bring it back to your breath. This can be done anywhere, whether you're sitting in a meeting or waiting in line at the grocery store. Another way to practice mindfulness is to bring your attention to your body. You can do a quick body scan, focusing on each part of your body in turn, noticing any sensations or feelings. This can be done sitting or standing, and can help you tune into your body and release tension. You can also practice mindfulness by simply paying attention to your surroundings. Take in the sights, sounds, and smells around you, without judgment or analysis. Whether you're walking, sitting, or doing everyday tasks, you can bring your full attention to the present moment and cultivate a sense of calm and awareness. In summary, mindfulness can be practiced anywhere, anytime, and by anyone. By bringing your attention to the present moment and cultivating a non-judgmental awareness, you can reduce stress, improve focus, and enhance overall well-being.

Incorporating mindfulness into daily life can help individuals to reduce stress and improve overall well-being. By cultivating a greater awareness of the present moment, individuals can develop a greater sense of calm, improve their ability to manage difficult emotions, and enhance their overall mental and physical health.

The philosophy behind mindfulness has its roots in ancient Buddhist teachings, particularly in the practice of meditation. Mindfulness is a core aspect of Buddhist practice and is believed to help individuals develop greater awareness and insight into the nature of reality, as well as to reduce suffering and cultivate greater well-being. The origins of mindfulness can be traced back to the teachings of the Buddha, who emphasized the importance of cultivating mindfulness as a means of achieving enlightenment. According to Buddhist philosophy, mindfulness involves paying attention to the present moment and becoming more aware of the nature of one's thoughts, feelings, and perceptions.

Since then, mindfulness has become increasingly popular as a tool for improving mental and physical health, with numerous research studies highlighting its benefits. While the practice of mindfulness has its roots in Buddhism, it has been adapted and integrated into secular contexts and is now practiced by people of various religious and cultural backgrounds. Overall, the philosophy behind mindfulness is based on the idea that by cultivating greater awareness and attention to the present moment, individuals can reduce suffering, improve well-being, and gain greater insight into the nature of their thoughts, feelings, and perceptions.

When starting a mindfulness practice, it's important to remember that it's a skill that requires regular practice to develop. You may find it difficult at first, and your mind may wander frequently, but with consistent practice, you can cultivate a greater sense of calm, awareness, and well-being.

Some additional tips for practicing mindfulness include:

1. Practice at the same time each day: This can help to establish a routine and make it easier to incorporate mindfulness into your daily life.

2. Be patient: It takes time to develop a mindfulness practice, so be patient and persistent.

3. Start small: Start with just a few minutes each day and gradually increase the length of your practice over time.

4. Take a course or seek guidance: If you're new to mindfulness, taking a course or seeking guidance from a mindfulness teacher or therapist can be helpful in establishing a practice and getting started.

Remember, the goal of mindfulness is not to eliminate thoughts or emotions, but to become more aware of them and develop greater clarity and insight into your experience. With regular practice, mindfulness can help you to develop a greater sense of calm, focus, and well-being.

CHAPTER THREE

Physical Exercise

A. Mental Benefits of Physical Exercise :

Physical exercise has numerous mental health benefits that can help to improve overall well-being. One of the most significant benefits is its ability to reduce stress and anxiety. When you exercise, your body releases endorphins, which are feel-good chemicals that can help to reduce feelings of anxiety, tension, and overwhelm. At the same time, physical activity has been shown to reduce levels of stress hormones like cortisol and adrenaline, which can contribute to a sense of calm and relaxation. Another benefit of exercise is its ability to improve mood. Research has found that people who exercise regularly tend to report higher levels of happiness, well-being, and self-esteem. This is likely due to the release of endorphins and other neurotransmitters that promote positive emotions. Additionally, the sense of accomplishment that comes with achieving fitness goals can help to boost self-confidence and provide a sense of purpose and meaning.

Regular exercise can also have a positive impact on cognitive function. Studies have shown that physical activity can help to improve memory, attention, and concentration, while also reducing the risk of cognitive decline and dementia. This is because exercise helps to promote the growth of new brain cells and increase blood flow to the brain, which can enhance neural function. In addition to these benefits, physical exercise can also be a powerful tool for managing symptoms of depression and other mental health conditions. Studies have shown that regular exercise can be as effective as medication in treating depression, and can also help to reduce symptoms of anxiety and improve overall quality of life. There is a significant body of scientific research that supports the mental health benefits of physical exercise. Here are some of the key findings:

1. Exercise can reduce stress and anxiety: Exercise has been shown to reduce levels of the stress hormone cortisol, which can contribute to feelings of anxiety and tension. Additionally, physical activity has been found to increase the production of endorphins and other feel-good chemicals in the brain, which can help to promote relaxation and reduce feelings of stress.

2. Exercise can improve mood: Numerous studies have shown that exercise can have a positive impact on mood, with regular physical activity being associated with reduced symptoms of depression and anxiety. The release of endorphins and other neurotransmitters during exercise is thought to play a significant role in this effect.

3. Exercise can boost cognitive function: Research has found that physical exercise can help to improve memory, attention, and other aspects of cognitive function. This is thought to be due to the promotion of neural growth and increased blood flow to the brain that occurs during exercise.

4. Exercise can reduce the risk of cognitive decline: Physical activity has been found to reduce the risk of cognitive decline and dementia in older adults, likely due to the positive impact on brain function.

5. Exercise can improve overall well-being: Regular physical activity has been associated with numerous positive outcomes, including improved sleep, increased energy, and a greater sense of purpose and meaning in life.

Overall, the scientific evidence strongly supports the mental health benefits of physical exercise. By incorporating regular physical activity into your routine, you can improve your mood, reduce stress and anxiety, boost cognitive function, and promote overall well-being.

The minimum daily physical activity level required for good mental health can vary depending on a number of factors, such as age, overall health, and fitness level. However, the World Health Organization (WHO) recommends that adults engage in at least 150 minutes of moderate-intensity aerobic physical activity per week, or at least 75 minutes of vigorous-intensity aerobic physical activity per week, in order to achieve health benefits.

In terms of mental health specifically, research has found that even small amounts of physical activity can have a positive impact. For example, a study published in the Journal of Psychiatric Research found that just 15 minutes of moderate-intensity exercise per day was associated with a 22% reduced risk of depression. Another study, published in the American Journal of Epidemiology, found that just 2.5 hours of moderate-intensity physical activity per week was associated with a 20% reduced risk of depression, and that the benefits were even greater for individuals who engaged in higher levels of physical activity.

Aim to engage in at least 30 minutes of moderate-intensity physical activity most days of the week, such as going for a brisk/fast walk. Over time, gradually increasing the duration and intensity of your physical activity can lead to even greater mental health benefits. For example, working up to a daily one hour-long brisk walk can be a great goal to strive for. Remember, any amount of physical activity is better than none, and finding enjoyable activities that you can incorporate into your daily routine can help make exercise a sustainable habit.

Summarizing, regular exercise has been shown to reduce symptoms of anxiety and depression, boost self-esteem, manage stress, and enhance cognitive function. Exercise can stimulate the release of endorphins and other "feel-good" chemicals in the brain, which can lead to improvements in mood and feelings of well-being. Engaging in physical activity can also provide a healthy outlet for stress and help individuals develop better coping mechanisms. Additionally, by setting and achieving exercise goals, individuals can improve their self-esteem and confidence. Finally, regular exercise has been linked to improved cognitive function, which can help individuals maintain their mental sharpness and reduce the risk of cognitive decline.

One way that daily physical exercise works as an immune system for mental health is by reducing stress and anxiety. Physical exercise triggers the release of endorphins, which are natural chemicals in the brain that promote feelings of happiness and relaxation. Exercise can also reduce levels of the stress hormone cortisol, which can help to lower overall levels of stress and anxiety. In addition to reducing stress and anxiety, daily physical exercise can also help to improve cognitive function and memory. Research has shown that exercise can improve blood flow to the brain, stimulate the growth of new brain cells, and enhance the connectivity between different regions of the brain. These changes can lead to improvements in cognitive function, such as attention, concentration, and memory. Furthermore, daily physical exercise can also help to promote better sleep. Regular exercise can help regulate the body's natural circadian rhythms, which can improve sleep quality and duration. Improved sleep can help protect against the negative effects of sleep deprivation, such as mood changes, cognitive impairment, and fatigue. Exercise can help to reduce the risk of chronic diseases such as obesity, diabetes, and heart disease, which can have negative effects on mental health. By promoting physical health, regular exercise can help to protect against the negative effects of physical illness on mental well-being.

Thus, daily physical exercise can work as an immune system for mental health by reducing stress and anxiety, improving cognitive function and memory, promoting better sleep, and improving overall physical health. By providing these benefits, regular exercise can help protect against mental health challenges and promote overall well-being.

B. How to Incorporate Exercise into Daily Routine :

Incorporating exercise into your daily routine can be a great way to improve your overall health and well-being. Here are a dozen ways to do so:

1. Set specific goals: Start by setting a specific goal for your exercise routine, such as exercising for 30 minutes a day or walking 10,000 steps. Write down your goal and keep it somewhere visible to remind you of it each day.

2. Start small: If you're new to exercise, start with something simple like a short walk around the block or a 10-minute yoga routine. Gradually increase the duration and intensity of your workouts as you get stronger.

3. Wake up early: Try setting your alarm 30 minutes earlier and use that extra time to exercise. Begin with a simple routine such as a morning stretch or light yoga session to wake your body up.

4. Take a walk during lunch break: Use your lunch break to go for a brisk walk around the block or nearby park. If you have limited time, try to take a shorter walk, even a few laps around the office can help.

5. Use the stairs: Instead of taking the elevator, use the stairs whenever possible. Start by taking the stairs for one or two floors and gradually increase the number of floors you climb each day.

6. Find an exercise buddy: Ask a friend or family member to join you in your exercise routine. This will help you stay motivated and accountable, and can make your exercise routine more fun and enjoyable.

7. Try a fitness class: Joining a fitness class can be a great way to stay motivated and try new types of exercise. Sign up for a class that interests you, and make it a priority to attend each week.

8. Use household items as exercise equipment: You don't need expensive equipment to exercise at home. Use household items like cans of food, water bottles, or a chair for bodyweight exercises. Try squats, lunges, or push-ups using a sturdy chair or bench.

9. Take a bicycle ride: If you have a bicycle, take it out for a ride around the neighbourhood. Start with a short ride and gradually increase the distance as you get more comfortable.

10. Do a quick workout during TV commercials: Instead of sitting on the couch during commercial breaks, use that time to do a quick workout. Try doing a few jumping jacks, push-ups, or lunges during each commercial break.

11. Park further away: When you go to the store or to work, park further away from the entrance. This will give you the opportunity to get some extra steps in throughout the day.

12. Get creative: There are many ways to incorporate exercise into your daily routine. Find something that works for you and make it a habit. It could be dancing while you're cooking dinner or doing some stretching while you're waiting for your coffee to brew. Make it a fun and enjoyable part of your day.

Remember to start slow, stay consistent, and gradually increase the duration and intensity of your exercise routine

C. Types of Exercises specifically for Mental Health :

There are different types of physical exercise that can be beneficial for mental health. Here are some of the 10 most common and beneficial types:

1. Aerobic exercise: This type of exercise, also known as cardiovascular exercise, includes activities such as running, cycling, swimming, and dancing. Aerobic exercise is known to boost the production of endorphins, which are chemicals in the brain that promote feelings of happiness and well-being. It can also reduce symptoms of anxiety and depression, improve cognitive function, and boost self-esteem. To reap the mental health benefits of aerobic exercise, aim for 30 minutes of moderate intensity exercise at least 3-5 times a week. To do it, start by finding an activity you enjoy, and gradually build up your intensity and duration over time. Here are some examples of aerobic exercises that can benefit mental health:

- Running or jogging: This is a great form of aerobic exercise that can improve cardiovascular health and boost mood. Running or jogging can be done outdoors or on a treadmill.

• Cycling: Cycling is a low-impact form of aerobic exercise that can improve mood and reduce stress. It can be done outdoors or on a stationary bike.

• Swimming: Swimming is a full-body workout that can help reduce anxiety and improve mood. It's a great form of exercise for people with joint pain or other physical limitations.

• Dancing: Dancing is a fun and social form of aerobic exercise that can improve mood and reduce stress. It can be done in a group class or at home with online videos.

• Walking: Walking is a simple and accessible form of aerobic exercise that can be done anywhere. It can help reduce symptoms of depression and anxiety and improve overall well-being.

• High-intensity interval training (HIIT): HIIT involves short bursts of intense exercise followed by periods of rest. It's a great way to improve cardiovascular fitness and boost mood.

2. Resistance training: This type of exercise involves using weights or resistance bands to strengthen and tone your muscles. Resistance training has been shown to have positive effects on mental health, including reducing symptoms of anxiety and depression, improving self-esteem, and enhancing cognitive function. Resistance training can also improve overall physical health, such as bone density and muscle mass. To reap the mental health benefits of resistance training, aim to do it at least 2-3 times per week. You can do this at home or at a gym with weights or resistance bands. Here are some examples of resistance training exercises that can benefit mental health:

• Weight lifting: Weight lifting involves lifting weights or using weight machines to target specific muscle groups. It can improve muscle strength and endurance, and can also enhance self-esteem and confidence.

• Bodyweight exercises: Bodyweight exercises such as push-ups, squats, and lunges use your own body weight for resistance. They can improve overall strength and mobility, and can be done anywhere without equipment.

• Resistance bands: Resistance bands are a versatile and portable form of resistance training that can be used to target specific muscle groups. They are a great option for people who don't have access to a gym or weight equipment.

3. Yoga: This type of exercise involves physical poses, breathing techniques, and meditation. Yoga has been shown to have many mental health benefits, including reducing symptoms of anxiety and depression, improving mood, and enhancing cognitive function. The combination of physical movement, deep breathing, and mindfulness helps to promote relaxation and reduce stress. To get started with yoga, find a local class or follow along with a video at home. There are many different types of yoga, so it's important to find a style that feels right for you. Here are some steps you can take to practice yoga for mental health:

• Set an intention: Before starting your yoga practice, set an intention for what you want to achieve. This could be to reduce stress, increase relaxation, or improve mood. This will help you stay focused and motivated throughout your practice.

• Choose a style of yoga: There are many different styles of yoga, each with its own benefits. Some styles that are particularly helpful for mental health include Hatha yoga, Restorative yoga, and Yoga Nidra. There are many poses in each type of yoga. Choose a style and pose that resonates with you and your goals.

• Find a comfortable space: Find a quiet, comfortable space where you can practice yoga without distractions. This could be a room in your home, a park, or a yoga studio.

• Use props: Yoga props such as blocks, straps, and blankets can help support your body and make poses more accessible. Use props as needed to make your practice more comfortable and effective.

• Focus on your breath: Throughout your yoga practice, focus on your breath. This can help calm your mind, reduce stress, and improve relaxation. Try to take slow, deep breaths, and synchronize your breath with your movements.

• Practice regularly: To experience the benefits of yoga for mental health, it's important to practice regularly. Try to practice yoga for at least 15-30 minutes a day, several times a week.

Here are three simple yoga exercises that can be beneficial for mental health and how to do them:

1. Child's pose: This is a gentle, calming pose that can help reduce stress and anxiety. How to do it: Start on your hands and knees with your wrists directly under your shoulders and your knees directly under your hips. Lower your hips back towards your heels and stretch your arms out in front of you. Rest your forehead on the floor and take slow, deep breaths. Hold the pose for 1-3 minutes.

2. Tree pose: This pose can help improve balance, focus, and concentration, while also reducing stress. How to do it: Stand with your feet hip-width apart and your arms at your sides. Shift your weight onto your left foot and lift your right foot off the ground. Place the sole of your right foot on your left thigh, with your toes pointing downwards. Keep your hands at your heart center or reach them towards the sky. Focus on a spot in front of you and hold the pose for 30-60 seconds. Repeat on the other side.

3. Corpse pose: This is a relaxing pose that can help reduce stress and promote relaxation. How to do it: Lie on your back with your arms at your sides and your palms facing up. Close your eyes and take slow, deep breaths. Allow your body to relax and sink into the ground. Hold the pose for 5-10 minutes, or as long as you like.

Remember to move slowly and mindfully into each pose, and listen to your body. If you experience any pain or discomfort, come out of the pose and rest. Practicing these yoga exercises regularly can help improve your mental health and overall well-being.

4. Tai Chi: This type of exercise involves slow, gentle movements that are coordinated with deep breathing and relaxation techniques. Tai Chi has been shown to have many mental health benefits, including reducing symptoms of anxiety and depression, improving mood, and enhancing cognitive function. The slow, deliberate movements and focus on mindfulness help to reduce stress and promote relaxation. To get started with Tai Chi, find a local class or follow along with any online video at home. While it's best to learn tai chi from a qualified instructor, it is possible to practice tai chi by yourself once you have a basic understanding of the movements. Here are some tips for practicing tai chi by yourself:

- Choose a quiet, comfortable space: Find a quiet, comfortable space where you can practice tai chi without distractions. This could be a room in your home, a park, or any other peaceful location.
- Start with a warm-up: Before starting your tai chi practice, warm up your muscles and joints with some gentle stretches or movements. This can help prevent injury and prepare your body for the practice.
- Focus on your breath: Throughout your tai chi practice, focus on your breath. Take slow, deep breaths and synchronize your breath with your movements. This can help calm your mind and reduce stress.
- Start with the basic movements: If you are new to tai chi, start with the basic movements and gradually build up to more advanced movements. The basic movements include the ward off, roll back, press, and push.
- Practice regularly: To experience the benefits of tai chi for mental health, it's important to practice regularly. Try to practice for at least 10-15 minutes a day, several times a week.

Here are some steps to practice a simple Tai Chi routine by yourself :

- Warm up with gentle stretches.
- Stand with your feet shoulder-width apart, knees slightly bent, and arms at your sides.
- Take slow, deep breaths and focus on your breath throughout the practice. Inhale as you raise your arms, and exhale as you push them down.

• Lift your arms up and push them down several times, synchronizing your breath with the movement.

• With your left hand at shoulder-height and your right hand at waist-level, shift your weight onto your left foot and turn to the left. Bring your right foot forward and push your right hand forward while pulling your left hand back. Inhale as you shift your weight, and exhale as you push and pull.

• Repeat this movement on the other side, and then repeat several times, alternating sides. Synchronize your breath with the movement.

• End by lifting your arms up and pushing them down one last time, synchronizing your breath with the movement.

Remember to move slowly and mindfully, and focus on your breath throughout the practice. Practice regularly, ideally for at least 10-15 minutes a day, several times a week.

5. Mindful walking: This type of exercise involves taking a walk while focusing on your senses and the present moment. Mindful walking has been shown to have many mental health benefits, including reducing symptoms of anxiety and depression, improving mood, and enhancing cognitive function. To do it, start by finding a quiet outdoor space where you can walk without distractions. Focus on the sensation of your feet touching the ground, the sights and sounds around you, and your breath.

Here are some steps to help you practice mindful walking:

1. Find a quiet and peaceful place: Find a place where you can walk without being distracted by traffic or other people.

2. Stand still and take a few deep breaths: Take a few deep breaths and center yourself before beginning your walk.

3. Begin walking slowly: Start by walking slowly and deliberately, taking small steps and placing your feet mindfully.

4. Focus on your breath: Focus your attention on your breath and the sensations in your body as you walk.

5. Be aware of your surroundings: Pay attention to your surroundings, noticing the colors, textures, and sounds around you.

6. Notice your thoughts and feelings: As thoughts and feelings arise, simply observe them without judgment or reaction. Bring your focus back to your breath and the present moment.

7. Practice gratitude: As you walk, cultivate a sense of gratitude for the opportunity to be present and alive.

8. Take your time: Continue walking mindfully, at your own pace, for as long as you like.

6. Dancing: This type of exercise involves rhythmic movements to music. Dancing has been shown to have many mental health benefits, including reducing symptoms of anxiety and depression, improving mood, and enhancing self-esteem. Dancing can also be a social activity, which can help to reduce feelings of isolation and improve social connections. To get started, find a local dance class or follow along with any online video at home. Here are some steps to help you practice dance to improve mental health:

1. Choose a type of dance: Choose a type of dance that you enjoy and that fits your mood. For example, if you want to release tension, you might choose a more energetic and expressive dance style like hip hop. If you want to relax, you might choose a more flowing and meditative dance style like contemporary or ballet.

2. Find a space to dance: Find a space where you can dance without being disturbed. You can use your living room, bedroom, or any other private space.

3. Put on some music: Choose music that matches the mood you want to create. You can use a music streaming service or create a playlist of your favorite songs.

4. Warm up: Before starting, warm up your body by stretching and moving your joints to avoid injury.

5. Move your body to the music: Let the music guide your movements and express your emotions through your body. Focus on your breath and the sensations in your body as you move.

6. Let go of self-judgment: Avoid judging yourself or worrying about how you look. Allow yourself to be free and let the movement flow.

7. Practice regularly: Dance regularly to make it a part of your self-care routine. You can start with short sessions of 10-15 minutes and gradually increase the time.

7. Pilates: This type of exercise focuses on strengthening the core muscles and improving posture. Pilates has been shown to have many mental health benefits, including reducing symptoms of anxiety and depression, improving mood, and enhancing cognitive function. The focus on breath and mindfulness in Pilates can also promote relaxation and reduce stress. To get started, find a local Pilates class or follow along with any online video at home. Here are some steps to help you practice Pilates :

- Find a comfortable and quiet space: Find a quiet and comfortable space in your home where you can lie down on a mat or a towel. It's also important to wear comfortable, breathable clothing that allows you to move freely.
- Warm up: Start by warming up your body with some gentle stretches and movements. You can start with some neck rolls, shoulder shrugs, and hip circles. This helps to prepare your body for the exercises to come and prevent injury.
- Focus on your breath: Pilates emphasizes the importance of deep, focused breathing. Begin by taking a few deep breaths and focus on breathing deeply into your diaphragm. As you perform each exercise, inhale deeply through your nose and exhale fully through your mouth. Focus on the rhythm of your breath and the way it connects your movements.
- Start with some basic exercises: Some simple exercises you can do include leg circles, the hundred, and the pelvic tilt. These exercises help to improve core strength, balance, and flexibility.

a. Leg circles: Lie on your back with your arms by your sides and your legs straight. Lift one leg up to the ceiling and make small circles with your foot, keeping your core engaged and your back flat on the mat. Switch legs and repeat.

b. The hundred: Lie on your back with your arms by your sides and your legs in a tabletop position. Lift your head, neck, and shoulders off the mat and pump your arms up and down vigorously for 100 counts, inhaling for 5 counts and exhaling for 5 counts.

c. Pelvic tilt: Lie on your back with your knees bent and your feet flat on the floor. Inhale deeply and as you exhale, engage your core and press your lower back into the mat, tilting your pelvis upward. Hold for a few seconds, then release.

• Progress to more challenging exercises: As you become more comfortable with the basic exercises, you can gradually progress to more challenging exercises such as the single-leg stretch, criss-cross, and the saw.

a. Single-leg stretch: Lie on your back with your knees bent and your feet flat on the floor. Lift one leg up to a tabletop position and hold it with both hands. Extend the other leg out straight, then switch legs, pulling your knee in toward your chest and extending the other leg out.

b. Criss-cross: Lie on your back with your hands behind your head and your knees bent. Lift your head, neck, and shoulders off the mat and twist your torso to one side, bringing your opposite elbow toward your knee. Switch sides and repeat.

c. The saw: Sit up tall with your legs stretched out in front of you and your arms out to the sides. Twist your torso to one side and reach your opposite arm toward your foot. Return to center, then twist to the other side and repeat.

• Cool down: After completing your Pilates routine, cool down by stretching your muscles and taking a few deep breaths. You can do some gentle stretches like hamstring stretches, quad stretches, and spinal twists.

• Practice regularly: To see the benefits of Pilates, it's important to practice regularly. You can start with 10-15 minutes a day and gradually increase the time as you become more comfortable.

8. Swimming: This type of exercise involves moving through water, either in a pool or natural body of water. Swimming has been shown to have many mental health benefits, including reducing symptoms of anxiety and depression, improving mood, and enhancing cognitive function. The buoyancy of water can also help to reduce stress on the joints and promote relaxation. Here are some steps to help you practice swimming for mental health:

- Set realistic goals: Start by setting achievable goals, such as swimming for 30 minutes, two to three times a week.
- Find a suitable location: Look for a swimming pool or open water location that is safe and convenient for you to access.
- Get the right gear: Make sure you have the appropriate swimming gear, including a comfortable swimsuit, goggles, and a swim cap if necessary.
- Warm up: Begin your swimming session with a few stretches and warm-up exercises to avoid any potential injuries.
- Practice different strokes: To keep your swim sessions interesting and challenging, practice different swimming strokes, such as freestyle, breaststroke, backstroke, and butterfly.
- Focus on breathing: Swimming can be an excellent way to practice mindfulness, so focus on your breathing while you swim. Take deep breaths and exhale slowly to calm your mind and body.
- Monitor your progress: Keep track of your progress by recording your swim times and distances. This can help you stay motivated and measure your progress over time.
- Take breaks as needed: Remember to take breaks as needed during your swim sessions, especially if you are just starting out. Listen to your body and avoid overexerting yourself.

9. Team sports: This type of exercise involves playing sports with others, such as soccer, basketball, or volleyball. Team sports have been shown to have many mental health benefits, including reducing symptoms of anxiety and depression, improving mood, and enhancing social connections. The social interaction during team sports can also promote a sense of belonging and reduce feelings of isolation. To get started, find a local team or recreational league.

Here are some steps on how to use team sports for mental health:

- Find a team sport that you enjoy: Look for a team sport that interests you, such as basketball, soccer, or volleyball. You can join a local recreational league or participate in pickup games with friends.
- Set realistic goals: Set achievable goals for yourself, such as attending regular team practices, improving your skills, or contributing to your team's success.
- Build relationships: Connect with your teammates by attending team practices and social events. Building positive relationships with others can boost your mood and reduce feelings of isolation.
- Focus on the present: Use team sports as a way to practice mindfulness by focusing on the present moment. Pay attention to your movements, your surroundings, and your team's performance.
- Exercise regularly: Team sports can provide a fun and engaging way to stay physically active. Regular exercise can help reduce stress, anxiety, and depression.
- Manage stress: Use team sports as a way to manage stress by taking time to relax and enjoy the game. Avoid placing too much pressure on yourself or your team's performance.

CHAPTER FOUR

Positive Self-Programming

A. What is positive self-programming?

Positive self-programming is the practice of consciously using positive words and phrases to affirm one's abilities, strengths, and potential. It is a cognitive-behavioral technique used in various fields such as sports, business, and psychology to enhance performance, build resilience, and promote well-being.

The concept of positive self-programming is based on the idea that one's thoughts and beliefs can affect their behavior, emotions, and outcomes. Positive self-programming is rooted in cognitive psychology, which suggests that one's thoughts and interpretations of events can influence their emotions and behaviors. By consciously using positive language and thoughts, individuals can train their minds to see situations in a positive light, which can lead to increased confidence, motivation, and better mental and emotional health. The scientific mechanism behind positive self-programming involves the way that thoughts and language affect the brain's neural pathways, which in turn impact emotions, behaviors, and outcomes. Positive self-programming can activate specific brain regions and alter the levels of neurotransmitters and hormones, resulting in various physiological and psychological effects.

When individuals engage in positive self-programming, they activate the prefrontal cortex, which is the part of the brain responsible for decision-making, problem-solving, and self-regulation. The prefrontal cortex has connections with other areas of the brain, such as the amygdala, which is responsible for processing emotions, and the hippocampus, which is involved in memory processing. Positive self-programming can help the prefrontal cortex regulate these areas of the brain, leading to improved emotional regulation and memory processing.

Positive self-programming can also increase the release of neurotransmitters such as dopamine, which is associated with motivation, reward, and pleasure. When individuals engage in positive self-programming, they may experience a sense of pleasure and reward, which can reinforce the behavior and lead to increased motivation and confidence. In addition to affecting neurotransmitters, positive self-programming can also impact hormones such as cortisol and oxytocin. Cortisol is a stress hormone that is released in response to perceived threats, while oxytocin is a hormone that is associated with social bonding and trust. Positive self-programming can reduce cortisol levels and increase oxytocin levels, leading to decreased stress and increased social connection. Another way that positive self-programming impacts the brain is through the process of neuroplasticity. Neuroplasticity refers to the brain's ability to adapt and change in response to new experiences and learning. When individuals engage in positive self-programming, they create new neural pathways in the brain that support positive emotions and behaviors. Over time, these neural pathways become stronger, leading to long-term changes in one's thought patterns and behaviors. Studies have shown that positive self-programming can have a significant impact on mental and emotional health. For example, research has found that individuals who engage in positive self-programming are less likely to experience symptoms of anxiety and depression. Positive self-programming can also improve self-esteem, increase motivation, and enhance overall well-being.

In addition to its psychological benefits, positive self-programming can also have physiological effects on the body. Studies have shown that positive self-programming can reduce stress and improve immune function. When individuals engage in positive self-programming, it can activate the body's relaxation response, leading to decreased heart rate, blood pressure, and muscle tension. Overall, positive self-programming is a powerful technique for enhancing performance, building resilience, and promoting well-being. By consciously using positive language and thoughts, and by activating specific brain regions, altering levels of neurotransmitters and hormones, and promoting neuroplasticity, individuals can train their minds to focus on the positive aspects of a situation, which can lead to improved mental and emotional health, increased motivation, and better overall outcomes. The scientific basis for positive self-programming lies in the brain's ability to change and adapt, and by engaging in positive self-programming, individuals can create new neural pathways that support positive emotions and behaviors.

Positive self-programming is an excellent coping mechanism because it can help you manage stress, anxiety, and depression by changing negative or self-critical thoughts into positive and empowering ones. Positive self-programming involves using encouraging, supportive, and realistic statements to help you reframe your thoughts and promote a more positive mindset. When faced with a stressful or challenging situation, our thoughts and emotions can quickly become negative and self-critical. Positive self-programming can help interrupt this negative cycle by promoting self-compassion, self-confidence, and self-motivation. It can also help you focus on your strengths and achievements rather than your weaknesses and failures.

B. How to Practice Positive Self-programming

There are several ways you can practice positive self-programming in your daily life. Here are some practical methods:

1. Identify negative self-programming: Start by noticing any negative self-programming that you have throughout the day. When you hear negative thoughts like "I'm not good enough," "I'm a failure," or "I can't do this," pause and challenge those thoughts.

Ask yourself if those thoughts are really true or if there is a more positive and realistic way to think about the situation.

Here are some practical ways to identify negative self-programming:

a. Pay attention to your inner voice: The first step in identifying negative self-programming is to pay attention to your thoughts. Throughout the day, take note of the thoughts that come into your head. Are they positive or negative? Are they helpful or harmful? This can help you become more aware of your self-programming patterns.

b. Look for patterns: Once you start paying attention to your thoughts, look for patterns in the situations or people that tend to trigger negative self-programming. For example, you may notice that you tend to engage in negative self-programming when you're around a certain person or when you're in a stressful situation.

c. Challenge your thoughts: When you notice negative self-programming, ask yourself if there is evidence to support that thought. Often, negative thoughts are not based in reality and are simply the result of our own negative biases or assumptions. For example, if you find yourself thinking "I‘m never going to be able to do this," ask yourself if there is any evidence to support that thought. Challenging negative thoughts can help you shift to a more positive mindset.

d. Use a thought record: A thought record is a tool used in cognitive-behavioral therapy to help identify negative thoughts and reframe them. To use a thought record, write down the negative thought, the situation that triggered it, and any evidence for or against the thought. Then, write down a more balanced and positive thought to replace the negative one. For example, if your negative thought is "I'm a failure because I didn't get the job," you might write down evidence that contradicts that thought (e.g. "I've gotten job offers in the past") and reframe the thought to be more positive (e.g. "I didn't get this job, but that doesn't mean I'm a failure. I'll keep trying"). The next chapter, i.e. journaling is about using thought record and it will guide you in great detail.

e. Seek feedback from others: Sometimes, we may not even realize we are engaging in negative self-programming. Seeking feedback from a trusted friend or therapist can help you identify negative thought patterns that you may not have been aware of. They can also offer alternative perspectives and help you reframe negative thoughts in a more positive light.

By using these techniques, you can become more aware of your negative self-programming and learn to reframe it in a more positive way. With practice, you can shift your mindset from one of self-criticism to one of self-compassion and positivity.

2. Reframe negative self-programming: To reframe negative self-programming, you need to identify the negative thoughts that are holding you back and find a way to reframe them in a positive way. For example, if you catch yourself thinking "I can't do this," try reframing the thought to "I may struggle, but I can figure this out with time and effort." When you notice negative self-programming, try to reframe those thoughts in a more positive light. For example, if you catch yourself thinking "I'm a failure," try reframing that thought to "I am learning and growing every day." This can help you shift your perspective and focus on the positive aspects of a situation rather than the negative.

Here are some practical ways you can practice to reframe negative self-programming:

a. Keep a thought diary: Write down your negative thoughts in a journal or notebook. Next to each negative thought, write a more positive and realistic thought that you can replace it with. This exercise will help you become more aware of your negative self-programming patterns and give you a tool to replace negative thoughts with more positive ones. Writing down your negative thoughts in a thought diary can help you become more aware of your negative self-programming patterns. For each negative thought, try to reframe it with a more positive and realistic thought. For example:

Negative thought: "I'll never be good at this"

Reframe: "I'm still learning, and I'm making progress. With practice and effort, I can improve."

b. Use positive affirmations: Write down positive affirmations on post-it notes and place them in places where you'll see them frequently, like on your bathroom mirror or computer monitor. Repeat them to yourself when you notice negative self-programming arising. Positive affirmations are statements that affirm positive qualities about yourself. They can help counteract negative self-programming and build self-confidence. Here are some examples of positive affirmations:

I am capable and competent

I am worthy of love and respect

I am resilient and can handle challenges

I am worthy of success and happiness

I am enough just as I am

c. Visualize success: When you have a negative thought, visualize yourself succeeding at the task or situation that the negative thought is related to. Imagine yourself feeling confident, capable, and successful. When you have a negative thought, visualize yourself succeeding at the task or situation that the negative thought is related to. Imagine yourself feeling confident, capable, and successful. For example:

Negative thought: "I'll never be able to give a good presentation"

Visualization: Close your eyes and imagine yourself giving a successful presentation. See yourself speaking confidently, engaging the audience, and receiving positive feedback.

d. Reframe the negative thought with evidence: When you have a negative thought, challenge it by asking yourself if there is any evidence to support it. Then, look for evidence that contradicts the negative thought. For example, if you have the thought "I'm a failure," look for evidence of times when you have succeeded. When you have a negative thought, challenge it by asking yourself if there is any evidence to support it. Then, look for evidence that contradicts the negative thought. For example:

Negative thought: "I‘m not good at anything"

Evidence: Think about your strengths and accomplishments. Write them down if it helps. For example, you may be a good listener, a talented artist, or a great cook.

e. Use humor: Use humor to reframe negative self-programming. For example, if you have the thought "I’m so stupid," say to yourself, "Well, at least I‘m smart enough to know when I’ve made a mistake." Using humor to reframe negative self-programming can help diffuse the negative emotion and shift your perspective. For example:

Negative thought: "I always mess up"

Reframe: "Well, at least I’m consistent!"

f. Practice self-compassion: Treat yourself with kindness and understanding. Instead of beating yourself up for your mistakes, offer yourself compassion and understanding. Remember that no one is perfect and that you are doing the best you can. Practicing self-compassion means treating yourself with kindness and understanding. Instead of beating yourself up for your mistakes, offer yourself compassion and understanding. For example:

Negative thought: "I can’t believe I made such a stupid mistake"

Self-compassion: "It’s okay to make mistakes. Everyone makes them. I'm still learning and growing."

g. Practice gratitude: Take time to focus on the things that you are grateful for. Write down three things that you are grateful for each day. This exercise can help shift your focus from negative self-programming to positive thoughts. Focusing on the things that you are grateful for can help shift your focus from negative self-programming to positive thoughts. Write down three things that you are grateful for each day.

Remember, the key is to practice these techniques consistently over time. The more you practice, the easier it will become to reframe negative self-programming and think more positively and constructively. Retraining your brain to think more positively takes time and practice. Be patient with yourself and keep practicing these techniques until they become a habit. Over time, you will find that your negative self-programming diminishes, and you are able to think more positively and constructively.

3. Use positive affirmations: Positive affirmations are statements that you can repeat to yourself to help shift your mindset towards a more positive outlook. Start by choosing one or two affirmations that resonate with you and repeat them to yourself throughout the day. You can say them out loud or silently in your head. Some examples of positive affirmations include "I am strong," "I am capable," or "I am worthy of love and respect." Choose a few positive statements that resonate with you and repeat them to yourself regularly. You can say them out loud or silently to yourself, and you can do it while looking in the mirror or while going about your day.

Positive affirmations can be a powerful tool for cultivating a positive mindset and building self-confidence. Here are some tips for using positive affirmations effectively:

a. Choose affirmations that resonate with you: The first step in using positive affirmations effectively is to choose affirmations that resonate with you. Affirmations should feel authentic and true to you in order to be effective. Start by identifying areas of your life where you would like to see positive changes. This might be related to self-esteem, career, relationships, health, or other personal goals. Once you have identified your areas of focus, think about the qualities you would like to cultivate in yourself. For example, if you want to build self-confidence, you might choose affirmations like "I am confident and capable" or "I trust myself and my abilities." If you want to improve your health, you might choose affirmations like "I am strong and healthy" or "I make healthy choices that nourish my body."

b. Use present tense and positive language: The second key to effective affirmations is to use present tense and positive language. Affirmations should be stated in the present tense, as if they are already true. This helps to reprogram your subconscious mind to believe that the desired outcome is already a reality. Using positive language also helps to create a positive and optimistic mindset. For example, instead of saying "I will be confident someday," say "I am confident and capable right now." Instead of saying "I won't fail," say "I am successful and capable of achieving my goals."

c. Repeat your affirmations regularly: The third key to effective affirmations is to repeat them regularly. Repetition helps to reinforce the positive beliefs you are trying to cultivate and make them a habit. Try repeating your affirmations first thing in the morning, before bed, or at any other time that feels comfortable for you. You can say them out loud or silently to yourself, whichever feels more natural. You can also try writing your affirmations down or using them as a mantra during meditation or mindfulness practices. The more you repeat your affirmations, the more they will become a natural part of your thinking and self-programming.

Overall, positive affirmations can be a powerful tool for cultivating a positive mindset and building self-confidence. By choosing affirmations that resonate with you, using present tense and positive language, and repeating them regularly, you can start to shift your thinking and beliefs in a more positive direction.

4. Practice gratitude: Practicing gratitude can help shift your focus to the positive aspects of your life. Each day, try to think of three things that you are grateful for. These can be small things like a good cup of coffee or a beautiful sunset, or larger things like a supportive friend or a fulfilling job. By focusing on the positive aspects of your life, you can help reduce negative self-programming and cultivate a more positive mindset. Keep a gratitude journal: To keep a gratitude journal, take a few minutes each day to write down things you are grateful for. This can help shift your focus away from negative thoughts and help you cultivate a more positive mindset.

Gratitude affirmations are covered in great detail in the second chapter of this book, which is one of the best ways to practise gratitude. Apart from that, here are few more effective ways through which one can practise gratitude :

a. Keep a gratitude journal: Every day, write down at least three things you're grateful for. It could be as simple as a good meal or a kind gesture from a friend. Writing them down helps you focus on the positive and reinforces the habit of looking for things to be grateful for.

b. Express your gratitude to others: Take the time to thank someone who has made a positive impact on your life. Write a note or send a message expressing your gratitude. You can also express gratitude in person by telling someone how much you appreciate them.

c. Take a gratitude walk: Take a walk outside and focus on the things you're grateful for. It could be the beauty of nature, the kindness of strangers, or the opportunities you've had in life.

d. Practice gratitude meditation: Sit in a quiet place and focus on the things you're grateful for. Breathe deeply and visualize these things in your mind. You can also repeat a gratitude mantra, such as "I am grateful for all the blessings in my life."

e. Use gratitude prompts: Use prompts to help you focus on specific things you're grateful for. For example, "I'm grateful for my health because..." or "I'm grateful for my job because..."

f. Practice gratitude in difficult situations: When faced with a challenging situation, try to find something to be grateful for. It could be a lesson you've learned or the support of loved ones. This can help shift your perspective and reduce stress.

g. Create a gratitude jar: Write down things you're grateful for on small pieces of paper and put them in a jar. Whenever you're feeling down, pull out a paper and read it to remind yourself of the good things in your life.

Let's take the example of keeping a gratitude journal. You can start by setting aside some time each day, such as right before bed or first thing in the morning, to write down at least three things you're grateful for. It can be helpful to be specific and reflect on why you're grateful for each item. For instance, "I'm grateful for my partner's support because they always listen to me and encourage me to pursue my dreams." Make this a daily habit, and over time, you'll start to notice the positive impact it has on your outlook.

Expressing gratitude to others can also be powerful. If you're not sure where to start, think about someone who has made a difference in your life. Write them a thank you note or send them a message expressing your gratitude. Be specific and share how their actions have impacted you. This not only makes the other person feel appreciated, but it also reinforces the habit of looking for things to be grateful for. In summary, practicing gratitude is all about focusing on the positive aspects of your life and developing a habit of gratitude. There are many ways to do this, so find the ones that work best for you and make them a part of your daily routine.

5. Use visualization: Visualization is a technique where you imagine yourself succeeding in a particular situation. This can help you build confidence and reduce negative self-programming. Imagine yourself feeling confident, capable, and successful. This can help you build a positive mindset and reduce self-doubt. To use visualization for positive self-programming, visualize yourself successfully achieving your goals, performing well in a job interview or presentation, or overcoming a difficult challenge. Here are some practical methods of using visualization:

a. Create a mental movie: Imagine a scenario where you feel confident, capable, and successful. Visualize yourself in vivid detail, from the way you're standing to the way you're speaking. Replay this mental movie in your mind whenever you need a boost of positivity. Example: If you're nervous about giving a presentation at work, imagine yourself giving the presentation with ease and confidence. Picture yourself speaking clearly, engaging your audience, and receiving positive feedback afterward.

b. Visualize positive self-programming: Imagine yourself saying positive affirmations to yourself, such as "I am capable," "I am confident," and "I am worthy." See yourself looking in the mirror and speaking these affirmations with conviction. Example: Before a job interview, visualize yourself standing in front of the mirror, saying positive affirmations to yourself, and feeling confident and prepared.

c. Use a vision board: Create a vision board with images and words that inspire you and represent your goals. Place it where you can see it every day, and take a few minutes to focus on it each morning. Visualize yourself achieving the goals represented on the vision board. Example: If your goal is to run a marathon, create a vision board with images of runners crossing the finish line, inspirational quotes about perseverance, and a map of the marathon route. Focus on the vision board each morning and imagine yourself completing the marathon with ease.

d. Visualization meditation: Close your eyes and imagine yourself in a peaceful and serene environment. It could be a beach, a forest, or a mountaintop. Visualize yourself feeling calm, relaxed, and at ease. Focus on positive thoughts and affirmations. Example: If you're feeling stressed and overwhelmed, visualize yourself in a peaceful forest, surrounded by trees and the sound of birds chirping. Focus on your breathing, and repeat positive affirmations to yourself, such as "I am calm, I am at peace, I am capable."

e. Visualize a successful outcome: Before attempting a task or project, take a few minutes to visualize yourself succeeding. Imagine everything going smoothly and according to plan, and feel the positive emotions associated with achieving your goal. Example: Before taking a test, visualize yourself confidently answering each question and receiving a high score. Feel the satisfaction and pride that comes with performing well.

In conclusion, there are many practical methods for using visualization to achieve positive self-programming. Experiment with different techniques and find the ones that work best for you. The key is to be consistent and make visualization a regular part of your routine.

6. Practice self-compassion: To practice self-compassion, treat yourself with the same kindness and care that you would offer to a close friend. Acknowledge your mistakes and limitations, but don't beat yourself up over them. Instead, offer yourself words of encouragement and support, and treat yourself with empathy and understanding.

Here are some practical methods to practice self-compassion, along with examples and explanations for each:

a. Talk to yourself like a kind friend: When you notice negative self-programming, imagine what you would say to a friend who was struggling with the same issue. Use the same gentle, encouraging tone with yourself that you would use with a friend. Example: If you make a mistake at work, instead of berating yourself and calling yourself names, imagine what you would say to a friend in the same situation. You might say, "It's okay, everyone makes mistakes. You'll learn from this and do better next time."

b. Practice mindfulness: When negative thoughts arise, try to observe them without judgment. Acknowledge the thought, but don't dwell on it or let it define you. Instead, focus on the present moment and your physical sensations. Example: If you notice a thought like "I'm so stupid," acknowledge the thought without judgment and redirect your attention to your physical sensations. You might say to yourself, "I notice the tension in my shoulders and the sensation of my feet on the ground."

c. Write a self-compassion letter: Write a letter to yourself from the perspective of a compassionate, understanding friend. Acknowledge your struggles and offer words of encouragement and support. Example: Write a letter to yourself acknowledging the difficulty of a recent breakup. Tell yourself that it's normal to feel sad and that you'll get through it. Offer words of encouragement, such as, "You're a strong person, and you have a lot of love and support in your life."

d. Practice self-care: Take care of your physical and emotional needs by doing things that make you feel good and nourished. This could be anything from taking a relaxing bath to going for a walk in nature. Example: Take a break from work and go for a walk outside. Breathe in the fresh air and notice the beauty of nature around you. Tell yourself that you deserve this break and that taking care of yourself is important. Or simply go on a vacation. Just don't consume illegal drugs like stupid teenagers.

Try out these methods and see which ones work best for you. The key is to be patient and gentle with yourself, and to remember that self-compassion is a journey, not a destination.

CHAPTER FIVE

Journaling

A. Introduction to Journaling

Journaling is a powerful self-care tool that involves regularly writing down your thoughts, feelings, and experiences in a notebook or electronic document. From a scientific perspective, journaling has been shown to have a number of mental health benefits. One of the main benefits is that it can help to reduce stress. Writing about your thoughts and feelings can provide a safe outlet for your emotions, which can help to reduce the physiological effects of stress on the body, such as elevated cortisol levels. In addition, journaling has been shown to improve mood and overall well-being. By writing about positive experiences and reflecting on your strengths and accomplishments, you can boost your self-esteem and cultivate a more positive outlook on life. From a neuroscience perspective, journaling works by engaging the prefrontal cortex, the part of the brain responsible for executive function and self-reflection. When you write about your thoughts and feelings, you are engaging in a form of self-reflection that can help to increase self-awareness and improve emotional regulation. Additionally, writing about traumatic experiences has been shown to reduce activity in the amygdala, the part of the brain responsible for fear and anxiety, which can help to reduce the intensity of negative emotions.

Journaling is a self-expression practice that involves regularly writing down your thoughts, feelings, and experiences. It is a highly versatile activity that can take many forms, from freeform writing to more structured prompts or guided exercises. Journaling has a number of benefits, including increased self-awareness. By taking the time to reflect on your thoughts and feelings, you can develop a greater understanding of your own inner world and gain insight into your emotions and behavior. Additionally, journaling can be a valuable tool for managing stress and promoting emotional regulation. Writing down your worries or concerns can help to provide a sense of release and perspective, while reflecting on positive experiences and accomplishments can help to boost self-esteem and foster a more positive outlook on life.

Journaling is a powerful tool that can serve as an effective immune system for mental health. Regular journaling can help to reduce stress, boost mood, increase self-awareness, and promote emotional healing. It allows individuals to process their thoughts, emotions, and experiences in a safe and private way. This process can help to identify patterns, triggers, and negative self-programming, allowing individuals to reframe their thoughts and develop more positive coping mechanisms. By promoting self-reflection, self-compassion, and self-growth, journaling can help to improve overall emotional wellbeing, strengthening the "immune system" of the mind. Additionally, journaling can be an effective tool for individuals undergoing therapy, as it can help to track progress, identify areas of concern, and explore new insights. By providing a safe and constructive outlet for emotions, journaling can be a valuable addition to any mental health regimen, helping individuals to build resilience, improve self-awareness, and cultivate a positive mindset.

B. Different Types of Journaling

There are many different types of journaling that you can try, depending on your goals and personal preferences. Here are the common types of journaling and how to do them:

1. Freeform Journaling: This is the most common type of journaling, where you simply write down your thoughts and feelings without any particular structure or prompt. This can be a great way to release your emotions, work through problems, or simply reflect on your day. To get started, set aside some time each day to write for at least 10-15 minutes. Write whatever comes to mind, without worrying about grammar or spelling.

Here's an example: "Today was a really stressful day at work. I had so many deadlines to meet and I felt like I couldn't keep up. I'm worried that I'm not doing a good job and that I'll get fired. But then I talked to my boss and she reassured me that I'm doing a great job. I feel a little better now, but I'm still anxious about everything I need to get done tomorrow."

Here are some simple steps to practice freeform journaling:

1. Set aside time: Choose a time and place where you can write without distraction. Set a timer for 10-15 minutes to give yourself a defined period of time to write.

2. Find a comfortable space: Choose a comfortable chair or a spot on the floor where you can write. Create an environment that feels welcoming and inspiring.

3. Start writing: Begin writing without worrying about structure or grammar. Write whatever comes to mind, allowing your thoughts to flow freely onto the page. Don't worry about making sense or being coherent.

4. Keep writing: If you get stuck or don't know what to write, keep writing anyway. Write about your surroundings, your emotions, your hopes and dreams, or anything that comes to mind.

5. Embrace the process: Don't worry about the quality of your writing. Remember that the purpose of freeform journaling is to let go of expectations and allow yourself to write without judgment.

6. Reflect on what you've written: After you've finished writing, take some time to reflect on what you've written. Consider what insights you've gained, what patterns you've noticed, and what emotions you've expressed.

7. Repeat: Practice freeform journaling regularly, aiming for a few times a week. Over time, you may find that this practice becomes an essential part of your self-care routine, helping you to

process your thoughts, manage stress, and connect with your inner self.

2. Gratitude Journaling: Gratitude journaling involves writing down things that you are thankful for, such as a positive experience, a kind word from a friend, or a beautiful sunset. This can be a powerful tool for cultivating a more positive outlook on life and promoting well-being. To get started, set aside a few minutes each day to reflect on something that you are grateful for, and write it down in your journal.

Here's an example: "Today I'm grateful for the warm sunshine on my face during my morning walk. It was so peaceful and refreshing, and it reminded me to slow down and enjoy the simple pleasures in life."

Here are some simple steps to practice gratitude journaling:

1. Set aside time: Choose a time and place where you can write without distraction. Set a timer for 10-15 minutes to give yourself a defined period of time to write.

2. Start writing: Begin by writing down things you are grateful for in your life. They can be big or small things, as long as they bring a feeling of gratitude.

3. Focus on the present: Try to focus on the present moment and write about things you are grateful for today.

4. Write in detail: Write in detail about why you are grateful for each item on your list. This can help you to feel more connected to the positive emotions associated with each item.

5. Be consistent: Try to make gratitude journaling a regular habit. Aim to write in your journal daily or a few times a week.

6. Use prompts: If you're having trouble getting started, try using prompts to help you generate ideas for things to be grateful for. Some examples of prompts include: "What made you smile today?", "What is something positive that happened this week?", or "Who are the people in your life that you are grateful for?"

7. Reflect on what you've written: After you've finished writing, take a moment to reflect on what you've written. Consider how the process of gratitude journaling made you feel and how it can impact your overall sense of well-being.

3. Dream Journaling: Dream journaling involves writing down your dreams each morning when you wake up. This can be a great way to gain insight into your subconscious mind and identify patterns in your dreams. To get started, keep a journal and pen by your bed, and write down your dreams as soon as you wake up, every time.

Here's an example: "Last night I had a dream that I was flying over a beautiful mountain range. It felt so exhilarating and free, and I didn't want the dream to end. I wonder if this dream has something to do with my desire for more freedom and adventure in my life."

Here are some simple steps to practice dream journaling:

1. Keep a journal and pen by your bed: Place a notebook and pen by your bed so that you can easily record your dreams as soon as you wake up.

2. Write immediately upon waking: Upon waking, write down everything you remember about your dream. Even if you only remember fragments or brief images, write them down.

3. Record details: Write down as many details as you can remember, such as the people, places, emotions, and actions that were present in the dream.

4. Use descriptive language: Use descriptive language to capture the sensory details of the dream, such as colors, sounds, and textures.

5. Draw pictures: If you're more of a visual person, consider drawing pictures to help you remember the details of your dreams.

6. Reflect on your dreams: Take some time to reflect on the dreams you've recorded. Look for patterns, recurring themes, or symbols that may be present in your dreams.

4. Reflection Journaling: Reflection journaling involves reflecting on a particular topic or question, such as "What are my goals for the next year?" or "What are my biggest strengths and weaknesses?" This can be a great way to gain clarity and insight into your own thoughts and feelings. To get started, choose a topic or question to reflect on, and write down your thoughts and ideas in your journal.

Here's an example: "What are my biggest strengths and weaknesses? I think my biggest strength is my ability to connect with people and make them feel comfortable. I'm also good at problem-solving and finding creative solutions. On the other hand, my biggest weakness is probably my tendency to procrastinate and get distracted easily. I need to work on being more focused and disciplined."

Here are some simple steps to practice reflection journaling:

1. Set aside time: Choose a time and place where you can write without distraction. Set a timer for 10-15 minutes to give yourself a defined period of time to write.

2. Choose a topic: Choose a specific experience, thought, or feeling that you want to reflect on in your journal. It can be a recent event, a personal challenge, or a recurring emotion.

3. Write freely: Start writing freely without worrying about grammar, spelling, or structure. Write down your thoughts and feelings as they come to you.

4. Ask yourself questions: As you write, ask yourself questions to help you reflect more deeply. Some examples of questions to ask yourself include: "What did I learn from this experience?", "How did I feel in this situation?", or "What could I have done differently?"

5. Find meaning: Look for meaning in your reflections. Consider what you've learned, how you can grow, and what changes you can make.

6. Be kind to yourself: Remember to be kind and compassionate to yourself as you reflect. Reflection is an opportunity to learn and grow, not to judge or criticize yourself.

7. Practice regularly: Make reflection journaling a regular habit. Try to write in your journal daily or a few times a week.

The most important thing is to find a type of journaling that resonates with you and that you enjoy, so that you can make it a regular habit and experience the many benefits of this powerful tool. When it comes to journaling, it's important to find a style or type of journaling that fits your interests and needs. Everyone has different preferences and goals, so what works for one person may not work for another. By trying different types of journaling, you can discover what resonates with you and what brings you the most enjoyment and benefit.

CHAPTER SIX

Social Support

A. Importance of Social Support

Social support refers to the various types of assistance and care that people receive from their social networks, such as family, friends, peers, and coworkers. This assistance can take many forms, including emotional support, practical assistance, and informational support. The importance of social support for mental health is well-documented in scientific research. One of the key ways that social support can help is by reducing feelings of isolation and loneliness, which are known to be risk factors for a range of mental health issues. Social support can also help individuals to build self-esteem and improve their sense of belonging, which can in turn promote positive mental health outcomes. In addition to these benefits, social support has also been shown to provide a buffer against the negative effects of stress on mental health. This is because when people have a supportive network of friends and family, they are better able to cope with stressful situations, which can in turn reduce the likelihood of developing mental health issues such as depression or anxiety. The scientific basis for social support's positive effects on mental health is rooted in a range of studies across a variety of different fields, including psychology, sociology, and neuroscience. For example, researchers have found that people who have higher levels of social support tend to have lower levels of stress hormones, such as cortisol. Additionally, social support has been shown to promote the release of feel-good hormones like oxytocin, which can help to reduce feelings of anxiety and depression.

There are many different ways to cultivate social support for mental health, including seeking out supportive relationships with family and friends, joining support groups, and engaging in activities that promote social connection, such as volunteering or participating in team sports. For those who are struggling with mental health issues, seeking out professional mental health services can also be an important way to build social support and access the care and resources needed to promote positive mental health outcomes. Overall, social support is an important factor in promoting positive mental health outcomes. Scientific research has demonstrated the many ways in which social support can help to reduce stress, improve self-esteem, and promote a sense of belonging, all of which can contribute to better mental health. If you are looking to improve your own mental health, seeking out social support from family, friends, and professionals can be a valuable step in achieving your goals.

Research has consistently shown that having positive social connections and a supportive social network can have a protective effect on mental health. For instance, studies have found that individuals with strong social support networks have lower rates of depression, anxiety, and stress, and are less likely to experience loneliness and social isolation. Conversely, social isolation and loneliness have been linked to negative mental health outcomes, such as increased risk of depression and anxiety.

So, just as the immune system is critical for protecting the body from harmful pathogens and infections, a supportive social network can help defend against mental health challenges. This is because social support can provide individuals with a range of resources, including emotional support, practical assistance, and a sense of belonging, all of which can help to buffer against stress and negative life events. For example, when an individual is going through a difficult time, such as the loss of a loved one, having a supportive social network can provide comfort, understanding, and a sense of being valued and cared for, which can help them to cope with the stress and feelings of grief. Similarly, having positive social connections can help to provide a sense of purpose and meaning, and can encourage individuals to engage in healthy behaviors and pursue positive goals, which can all contribute to better mental health. In summary, having a social support network can act as an immune system for mental health by providing protective factors against stress and negative life events, promoting positive coping strategies, and enhancing overall well-being.

B. Building a Social Support Network

Building a social support network can take time and effort, but it is a worthwhile investment in your mental and emotional health. Here are some steps you can take to build a social support network:

1. Identify your needs: Before you start building your social support network, it is essential to identify your needs. What kind of support do you need? Do you need emotional support, practical support, or both? Do you want someone to talk to, or do you need help with tasks or errands? Knowing what you need will help you identify the type of people you want in your support network. Here are some steps you can take to identify your needs:

a. Reflect on your current situation: Take some time to think about what's going on in your life right now. Are you facing any challenges or struggles? What areas of your life could use some support? This could be anything from emotional support to practical help with tasks.

b. Consider your strengths and weaknesses: Think about your own strengths and weaknesses. What are you good at, and where do you struggle? This can help you identify areas where you might need extra support.

c. Think about the type of support you need: There are different types of support, including emotional, informational, and practical support. Emotional support involves having someone to talk to and confide in, while informational support involves receiving advice or information from others. Practical support involves help with specific tasks, such as running errands or childcare. Think about which type of support would be most helpful to you.

d. Identify potential sources of support: Think about the people in your life who could provide you with support. This could include friends, family members, colleagues, or members of a support group. Consider their strengths and weaknesses, and think about whether they would be a good fit for the type of support you need.

2. Reach out to friends and family: Your existing friends and family can be a good place to start building your support network. Reach out to those you feel comfortable talking to and let them know you would like to build a stronger connection. If you have lost touch with some of your friends and family, consider reaching out to them and rekindling your relationship. Here are some tips for reaching out to your support network:

a. Be clear about what you need: Before reaching out, make sure you're clear about what type of support you're looking for. This will help you communicate your needs more effectively to others and make it easier for them to provide the help you need.

b. Choose the right time and place: Choose a time and place where you can have a conversation without interruptions. This will help ensure that you have the person's undivided attention and can discuss your needs without distractions.

c. Be honest and open: When you're reaching out to your support network, it's important to be honest and open about what you're going through. Share your feelings and concerns, and let them know how they can help.

d. Be specific: Provide specific examples of how others can support you. For example, if you need emotional support, you might ask for someone to listen to you without judgment or offer words of encouragement. If you need practical support, you might ask for help with specific tasks or errands.

e. Listen to their response: When you reach out for support, it's important to be open to the response you receive. Your friends and family may have their own needs or limitations, and it's important to be respect their boundaries. Listen to their response and be open to finding a solution that works for both of you.

f. Follow up: Once you've reached out for support, follow up with your friends and family to let them know how you're doing and whether their support has been helpful. This will help strengthen your relationships and show them that you appreciate their support.

3. Join social groups: Joining social groups can be a great way to meet new people who share your interests. Consider joining a club or group related to your hobbies or passions. This can be a great way to connect with people who have similar interests and may be able to provide emotional support when needed. Here are some tips for finding and joining social groups:

a. Identify your interests: Start by identifying your interests and hobbies. What activities do you enjoy doing? What topics are you passionate about? This will help you find groups that align with your interests.

b. Research social groups: Once you've identified your interests, research social groups in your community that focus on those interests. You can use social media, online search engines, or community bulletin boards to find groups. You can also ask your friends and family if they know of any groups that might be a good fit for you.

c. Attend events: Attend events hosted by social groups that you're interested in. This will give you the opportunity to meet the members and get a feel for the group's dynamics. Some events may be free, while others may require payment, so be sure to check ahead of time.

d. Introduce yourself: When you attend events, be sure to introduce yourself to the members. Let them know that you're interested in joining the group and ask any questions you may have. This is a good way to start building relationships with the members.

e. Participate in activities: Once you've joined a social group, be sure to participate in the activities and events. This will give you the opportunity to interact with the members and build relationships with them.

f. Be open and friendly: When you're trying to create a social support network, it's important to be open and friendly with the members of the group. This will make it easier for them to get to know you and provide support when you need it.

g. Follow up: After attending events or participating in activities, follow up with the members. This can be as simple as sending a quick message to say that you enjoyed meeting them or that you're looking forward to the next event. Following up will help you maintain the relationships you've built and stay connected with the group.

4. Consider volunteering: Volunteering can be a great way to meet new people while giving back to the community. It can also be a way to develop new skills and build your self-confidence. Here are some tips for finding and participating in volunteering opportunities:

a. Identify your interests: Start by identifying the causes that are important to you. What issues or problems do you care about? What skills or expertise do you have that could be useful in a volunteering role?

b. Research volunteer opportunities: Once you've identified your interests, research volunteer opportunities in your community that align with those interests. You can use online search engines, volunteer databases, or contact local organizations to find out about opportunities.

c. Choose the right role: When choosing a volunteering role, look for opportunities that match your skills and interests. This will make it more likely that you'll enjoy the work and be able to make a meaningful contribution.

d. Participate in training: Many volunteering opportunities will provide training or orientation sessions to help you get started. Be sure to attend these sessions to learn more about the organization and the role you'll be playing.

e. Connect with other volunteers: When you're volunteering, take the opportunity to connect with other volunteers. This can help you build relationships and a sense of community within the organization.

f. Be reliable: When you're volunteering, it's important to be reliable and consistent. Be sure to show up on time and complete the tasks assigned to you. This will help build trust with the organization and the other volunteers.

g. Follow up: After volunteering, be sure to follow up with the organization and other volunteers. This can be as simple as sending a thank-you note or expressing your interest in future volunteering opportunities. Following up will help you stay connected with the organization and the people you've worked with.

h. Take care of yourself: Volunteering can be rewarding, but it's important to take care of yourself as well. Make sure you're taking breaks, eating well, and getting enough rest. This will help you be more effective in your volunteering role and better able to provide support to others.

5. Seek professional support: If you are struggling with mental health issues or other personal challenges, seeking professional support can be a crucial part of building your support network. A therapist or counselor can provide you with emotional support and help you develop coping strategies. A therapist or counselor can provide a safe and supportive space for you to explore your feelings, thoughts, and experiences related to social support. They can help you identify any obstacles or challenges that might be preventing you from building a support network, and work with you to develop strategies for overcoming them. Additionally, a therapist or counselor can provide you with guidance and feedback as you work to build and maintain relationships with family and friends.

Here are some ways that a therapist or counselor can support you in building a social support network:

a. Identify your needs: A therapist or counselor can help you identify your social support needs and the types of relationships that you are looking for. For example, you may need emotional support, practical support, or a combination of both. They can also help you understand your attachment style, which can impact how you form and maintain relationships.

b. Develop a plan: Once you've identified your needs, a therapist or counselor can help you develop a plan for building a support network. This might include identifying people in your life who can provide different types of support, setting goals for building and maintaining relationships, and exploring new social activities or groups that align with your interests.

c. Address any obstacles: Sometimes, there may be obstacles that are preventing you from building a support network. For example, you may have social anxiety or a history of trauma that makes it challenging to connect with others. A therapist or counselor can help you work through these obstacles and develop strategies for managing them.

d. Practice communication skills: Communication is an important part of building and maintaining relationships. A therapist or counselor can provide you with guidance on how to communicate effectively, listen actively, and set boundaries. They can also help you practice these skills in a safe and supportive environment.

e. Provide support: Building a social support network can be challenging and may involve some setbacks or disappointments along the way. A therapist or counselor can provide you with support and encouragement as you work towards your goals. They can also help you process any feelings of loneliness or social isolation that you may be experiencing.

6. Attend events and gatherings: Attending events and gatherings, such as parties, conferences, or community events, can be a great way to meet new people and build connections. Be open to starting conversations and getting to know new people. Here are some suggestions:

a. Attend public events: Attending public events, such as concerts, art exhibits, or community festivals, is a great way to meet new people and connect with others who share similar interests. You can look for these events in your community by checking local newspapers or event calendars, or by searching online for event listings. Once you've found an event that interests you, make an effort to strike up conversations with the people you meet. You can start by asking about their opinions on the event or the artist, and then move on to other topics that interest you.

b. Take a class: Taking a class or workshop is a great way to learn something new while also meeting new people. You can look for classes or workshops in your community by checking local community centers, colleges, or adult education programs. You can also search online for classes that interest you. Once you've found a class, make an effort to introduce yourself to your classmates and strike up conversations before and after class. You can also suggest forming a study group or meeting up for a practice session outside of class.

c. Attend networking events: Networking events are a great way to connect with others who share your career goals or interests. You can look for networking events in your industry or profession by checking online event listings or professional association websites. Once you've found a networking event, prepare a brief introduction of yourself and your interests or career goals. Make an effort to introduce yourself to others and ask about their work or interests. You can also follow up with a thank-you email or message after the event to continue the connection.

d. Attend Meetup groups: Meetup is an online platform that connects people with similar interests who want to meet up in person. You can join or create Meetup groups based on your interests and attend events with other members. To get started, search for Meetup groups in your area and join those that interest you. Once you've joined a group, make an effort to attend events and introduce yourself to other members. You can also suggest hosting your own event or activity if there isn't already one planned that aligns with your interests.

e. Host your own event: If you're not receiving invitations to events, consider hosting your own. You can host a potluck dinner, a game night, a book club meeting, or any other type of gathering that interests you. Invite people you know, or post the event on social media or online platforms to attract new people. Make an effort to introduce everyone at the event and provide activities or conversation topics to help everyone feel comfortable and engaged.

7. Join online communities: Online communities can be a great way to connect with like-minded people who share your interests or challenges. You can join online support groups, forums, or social media groups related to your interests, hobbies, or mental health. Just remember to be cautious about sharing personal information online and seek help from professionals if you need it. Here are some steps you can take to join online communities:

a. Identify your interests: Think about the topics or activities that interest you, and search for online communities that revolve around those interests. This could include groups on social media platforms like Facebook or LinkedIn, forums or discussion boards, or specialized communities on platforms like Reddit.

b. Join relevant groups: Once you've identified some online communities that interest you, join them! Many groups will require you to request membership or answer a few questions before joining, so be prepared to provide some basic information about yourself. Make sure to read the group's rules and guidelines before posting to ensure that you're following the community's expectations.

c. Engage with the community: Once you've joined a community, start engaging with the other members. This could include posting questions, responding to others' posts, or starting conversations around shared interests. Try to be respectful and mindful of others' perspectives, and avoid engaging in any negative or confrontational behavior.

d. Attend virtual events: Many online communities will host virtual events like webinars, Q&A sessions, or virtual hangouts. Attend these events when possible, as they can be a great way to connect with other members and build relationships.

e. Build relationships outside of the community: If you connect with someone in an online community, consider reaching out to them outside of the group. You could send them a private message, connect on social media, or even arrange a video call to get to know them better.

8. Participate in group activities: Participating in group activities, such as team sports, dance classes, or book clubs, can be a great way to meet new people and build a sense of community. You can also consider hosting your own events, such as potluck dinners or game nights, to bring people together. Here are some examples of how you can participate in group activities to build a social support network:

a. To participate in group activities for social support network building, start by identifying your interests and researching group activities in your area that align with those interests. Examples of group activities could include joining a yoga or meditation group, participating in a community service group, attending cultural events, joining a sports club, joining a book club, or taking a cooking class.

b. Once you've found a group activity that interests you, attend their events and activities to get to know other members and start building connections. For example, if you join a sports club, attend their games and practices to meet other members and get involved in the group.

c. To build stronger relationships with other members, participate in group activities and offer to help with any tasks or projects the group may have. For example, if you join a community service group, volunteer to help with their upcoming event or project to show your commitment and build connections with other members.

d. Be open and approachable: Be open to meeting new people and approachable to others who may want to connect with you. Strike up conversations with other members and actively engage with the group.

e. Show up consistently: Attend group activities on a regular basis to show your commitment and build relationships with other members.

9. Be a good listener: Building strong relationships requires mutual support and understanding. Make sure you listen actively to others when they share their problems, and be there for them when they need your support. Being a good listener can also help you build trust and rapport with others. Here are some tips to help you become a good listener:

a. Give your full attention: When someone is speaking to you, give them your full attention. Avoid distractions such as checking your phone or looking around the room, and maintain eye contact with the speaker.

b. Show empathy: Try to put yourself in the speaker's shoes and understand their point of view. Show empathy by acknowledging their feelings and responding in a supportive way.

c. Avoid interrupting: Interrupting the speaker can make them feel unheard and frustrated. Allow the speaker to finish their thoughts before responding or asking questions.

d. Ask open-ended questions: Ask open-ended questions to encourage the speaker to elaborate on their thoughts and feelings. This can help you better understand their perspective and build a deeper connection with them.

e. Practice active listening: Active listening involves actively engaging with the speaker by providing feedback and reflecting on what they have said. Paraphrase what the speaker has said to ensure that you have understood their message correctly.

f. Be patient: Being a good listener requires patience and an open mind. Allow the speaker to express their thoughts and feelings at their own pace, without feeling rushed or judged.

In summary, building a social support network involves identifying your needs, reaching out to friends and family, joining social groups, volunteering, seeking professional support, attending events, and being patient. Remember that building a support network takes time and effort, but it is worth it for your mental and emotional well-being. Building a social support network is a continuous process, and it requires time, effort, and patience. Don't be afraid to reach out to others, and be willing to give as well as receive support. Don't be afraid to step outside of your comfort zone and try new things, and be open to meeting people who may be different from you. By putting yourself out there and actively seeking out opportunities to connect, you can build a strong and supportive social network.

C. Overcoming common barriers

While building a social support network, several barriers can arise that can make it challenging to establish and maintain relationships. Here are some common barriers and strategies for overcoming them:

1. Fear of rejection: Many people are hesitant to reach out to others because they fear rejection or judgment. To overcome this barrier, it's important to remember that building relationships takes time and effort. Don't take it personally if someone declines your invitation or doesn't respond immediately. Keep trying and focus on building genuine connections with people who share your values and interests.

Firstly, it is important to understand that rejection is a natural part of human interaction, and everyone experiences it at some point. Recognize that rejection is not a reflection of your worth as a person, but rather a mismatch in expectations or needs.

To overcome the fear of rejection, start by setting realistic goals for social interactions. Start small by reaching out to acquaintances or colleagues, and gradually work your way up to forming deeper connections. Practice active listening, and ask open-ended questions to show your interest in others. Additionally, focus on building self-confidence and resilience. Engage in activities that make you feel good about yourself, and challenge negative self-programming by reframing your thoughts. Remind yourself of your positive qualities and experiences and celebrate small victories. Finally, it's important to remember that not everyone will be a good fit for your social support network. Instead of dwelling on rejection, learn from it and keep moving forward. Recognize that building a support network takes time, effort, and patience, but the rewards are worth it.

2. Lack of time: Many people lead busy lives, and it can be difficult to find time to socialize. To overcome this barrier, try to prioritize social activities in your schedule. Set aside time each week to connect with friends or attend social events. You can also consider combining social activities with other tasks, such as exercising or running errands.

Firstly, assess how you currently use your time and identify areas where you can make adjustments. Look for small pockets of time, such as during your commute or lunch break, that you can use to reach out to others. Consider scheduling regular social activities, like a weekly lunch or coffee break, that fit into your schedule.

Secondly, consider the quality of the time you spend with others. It is better to have a few close relationships than many superficial ones. Focus on building meaningful connections with people who share your interests and values. This can often be achieved by joining a club or group centered around a hobby or passion.

Thirdly, consider using technology to maintain and strengthen your social connections. Social media platforms, email, and video calls can provide a convenient way to stay in touch with friends and family. However, it is important to balance virtual connections with face-to-face interactions.

Finally, consider delegating some of your responsibilities or tasks to create more time for social activities. This can involve hiring a cleaner, using grocery delivery services or working with a virtual assistant. Remember, building a social support network is a crucial part of a healthy and fulfilling life, and it is worth prioritizing even when time is limited.

3. Lack of confidence: Low self-esteem or social anxiety can make it difficult to initiate or maintain relationships. To overcome this barrier, it's important to work on building your self-confidence. Start with small, manageable social situations, and gradually challenge yourself to engage in more challenging interactions. Seek support from a therapist or counselor if necessary. Here are some practical steps you can take:

a. Identify and challenge negative self-programming: Negative self-programming can be a significant barrier to building confidence. Start by identifying negative thoughts you have about yourself and challenge them with positive affirmations. For example, if you think "I'm not interesting enough to make friends," challenge that thought by reminding yourself of your positive qualities.

b. Take small steps to expand your comfort zone: Building confidence requires taking small steps to expand your comfort zone. Start by engaging in low-risk social situations, such as joining a group that shares your interests or attending a social event with a friend. As you become more comfortable, gradually challenge yourself to step out of your comfort zone.

c. Focus on giving to others: One effective way to build confidence is to focus on giving to others. By volunteering or helping others, you can gain a sense of purpose and accomplishment that can boost your self-esteem.

d. Practice self-care: Taking care of yourself is crucial to building confidence. Make sure to get enough sleep, exercise, and eat a healthy diet. Engage in activities that you enjoy and that make you feel good about yourself.

e. Seek support: Finally, don't be afraid to seek support from others. Reach out to trusted friends or family members for encouragement and support. Consider seeking the help of a therapist or counselor if you are struggling with severe lack of confidence.

4. Geographical barriers: Living in a remote area or having limited mobility can make it challenging to build a social support network. To overcome this barrier, consider joining online communities or social media groups related to your interests. You can also seek out local support groups or volunteer opportunities to connect with others in your community.

5. Cultural or language barriers: Differences in language or cultural background can make it challenging to establish relationships with people from diverse backgrounds. To overcome this barrier, try to learn about other cultures and be respectful of differences. Seek out opportunities to connect with people from diverse backgrounds, such as attending cultural events or joining international clubs.

6. Past negative experiences: Previous negative experiences, such as rejection or betrayal, can make it challenging to trust others and build new relationships. To overcome this barrier, it's important to work through past traumas with the help of a therapist or counselor. Take your time and focus on building relationships with people who demonstrate trustworthiness and respect.

Remember, building a social support network takes time and effort, but it can be a valuable source of emotional and practical support. Be patient and persistent, and don't be afraid to seek support from professionals or loved ones along the way.

CHAPTER SEVEN

Breathing exercises

Breathing exercises are a simple and effective way to improve mental health and reduce stress and anxiety. Here are some breathing exercises that will help :

1. Deep Breathing: This technique involves breathing deeply and slowly, taking long breaths in through the nose and out through the mouth. Focus on feeling your diaphragm expand and contract as you inhale and exhale. There is both psychological and neurological evidence to support the benefits of deep breathing.

Psychologically, deep breathing helps reduce stress and anxiety by activating the parasympathetic nervous system, which is responsible for the "rest and digest" response. This response helps to slow down the heart rate, decrease blood pressure, and reduce the levels of stress hormones such as cortisol in the body. Neurologically, deep breathing increases the activity in the prefrontal cortex of the brain, which is responsible for executive functions such as decision making, attention, and working memory. Deep breathing also decreases the activity in the amygdala, which is responsible for the fear response. This leads to a decrease in anxiety and an increase in relaxation.

Studies have also shown that deep breathing can increase heart rate variability, which is a measure of the flexibility of the autonomic nervous system. Higher heart rate variability is associated with better mental and physical health. Overall, deep breathing is a simple yet effective technique for improving mental health and reducing stress. By activating the parasympathetic nervous system and increasing activity in the prefrontal cortex, it can help promote relaxation and reduce anxiety. Here's how to do deep breathing effectively:

a. Find a quiet and comfortable place to sit or lie down.

b. Close your eyes and take a few slow and deep breaths in through your nose and out through your mouth to help you relax.

c. Place one hand on your chest and the other on your stomach.

d. Inhale slowly and deeply through your nose, letting your stomach rise as you breathe in. Try to breathe into your abdomen, not just your chest.

e. Hold your breath for a few seconds, then exhale slowly and deeply through your mouth, letting your stomach fall as you breathe out.

f. Repeat this process for several minutes, focusing on your breath and clearing your mind of other thoughts.

g. Gradually increase the duration of your deep breathing sessions as you become more comfortable with the practice.

h. Deep breathing can be done anytime and anywhere, and it can help to reduce stress, anxiety, and tension. By practicing deep breathing regularly, you can improve your sleep quality and overall well-being.

2. Equal Breathing (Sama Vritti): In this technique, you inhale for a count of four, hold your breath for a count of four, and then exhale for a count of four. Repeat this pattern for several minutes, focusing on the rhythm of your breath. Equal breathing, also known as sama vritti or box breathing, is a breathing technique that involves inhaling and exhaling for the same length of time. Like deep breathing, equal breathing can have psychological and neurological benefits that can improve mental health.

Psychologically, equal breathing can help to reduce anxiety and improve focus. By regulating the breath, it helps to calm the mind and reduce feelings of stress. This can improve the ability to focus and concentrate on tasks, which can be helpful for people who suffer from anxiety or attention-related disorders. Neurologically, equal breathing can help to regulate the autonomic nervous system, which is responsible for regulating bodily functions such as heart rate, digestion, and breathing. By practicing equal breathing, it can help to balance the activity of the sympathetic nervous system, which is responsible for the body's stress response, and the parasympathetic nervous system, which is responsible for the body's rest and digest response. This can help to reduce the physical symptoms of stress, such as elevated heart rate and blood pressure. Equal breathing can also increase the flow of oxygen to the brain, which can improve cognitive function and overall mental clarity. It can also increase the activity of the prefrontal cortex, which is responsible for executive functions such as decision making and working memory. In summary, equal breathing can have psychological and neurological benefits that can improve mental health by reducing anxiety, improving focus, and regulating the autonomic nervous system.

Here's how to do equal breathing effectively:

a. Find a quiet and comfortable place to sit or lie down.

b. Breathe in slowly and deeply through your nose for a count of four.

c. Hold your breath for a count of four.

d. Breathe out slowly and completely through your mouth for a count of four.

e. Hold your breath for a count of four.

f. Repeat this process for several minutes, focusing on your breath and clearing your mind of other thoughts.

g. Gradually increase the duration of your equal breathing sessions as you become more comfortable with the practice.

3. Belly Breathing: Belly breathing, or diaphragmatic breathing, is a technique that involves breathing deeply into the belly. Studies have shown that this technique can have both psychological and neurological benefits that can improve mental health.

Psychologically, belly breathing can help to reduce anxiety and improve mood. One study found that practicing diaphragmatic breathing can decrease feelings of anxiety and improve mood in adults (Ritz et al., 2013). Another study found that this technique can help reduce symptoms of depression in individuals with chronic obstructive pulmonary disease (Pursnani et al., 2016).

Neurologically, belly breathing can help to regulate the autonomic nervous system and the hypothalamic-pituitary-adrenal (HPA) axis, which is the body's stress response system. One study found that practicing diaphragmatic breathing can reduce sympathetic nervous system activity and increase parasympathetic nervous system activity, which can help to reduce the physical symptoms of stress (Pal et al., 2004). Another study found that diaphragmatic breathing can decrease cortisol levels, a stress hormone that can lead to negative effects on mental health (Ma et al., 2017). Belly breathing can also increase the flow of oxygen to the brain, which can improve cognitive function and overall mental clarity. One study found that diaphragmatic breathing can increase cerebral blood flow, which can improve cognitive performance (Yuan et al., 2018). It can also increase the activity of the prefrontal cortex, which is responsible for executive functions such as decision making and working memory (Streeter et al., 2017).

Overall, scientific literature and research suggest that belly breathing can have psychological and neurological benefits that can improve mental health by reducing anxiety, improving mood, and regulating the body's stress response system. I have quoted the relevant scientific literature to establish the factual and scientific accuracy of the content.

Here's how to do belly breathing effectively:

a. Find a quiet and comfortable place to sit or lie down.

b. Place one hand on your chest and the other on your belly.

c. Inhale slowly and deeply through your nose, letting your belly rise as you breathe in. Try to breathe into your abdomen, not just your chest.

d. Hold your breath for a few seconds.

e. Exhale slowly and completely through your mouth, letting your belly fall as you breathe out.

f. Repeat this process for several minutes, focusing on your breath and clearing your mind of other thoughts.

g. Gradually increase the duration of your belly breathing sessions as you become more comfortable with the practice.

4. Alternate Nostril Breathing: This technique involves breathing in through one nostril and out through the other, alternating between each nostril. This can help balance the nervous system and reduce stress. Alternate nostril breathing, also known as Nadi Shodhana or Anulom Vilom, is a breathing technique that involves alternating between the nostrils while breathing. This technique can have psychological and neurological benefits that can improve mental health.

Psychologically, alternate nostril breathing can help to reduce stress and anxiety, as well as improve mood and cognitive function. One study found that practicing this technique can decrease symptoms of anxiety and improve cognitive performance in individuals with hypertension (Kjellgren et al., 2007). Another study found that it can improve mood and decrease feelings of stress in healthy adults (Telles et al., 2013). Neurologically, alternate nostril breathing can help to balance the activity of the sympathetic and parasympathetic nervous systems, which can help to regulate the body's stress response system. One study found that this technique can increase parasympathetic nervous system activity and decrease sympathetic nervous system activity, leading to reduced heart rate and blood pressure (Telles et al., 2010). Another study found that it can decrease cortisol levels, a stress hormone that can lead to negative effects on mental health (Mondal et al., 2012). Alternate nostril breathing can also increase the flow of oxygen to the brain, which can improve cognitive function and overall mental clarity. One study found that it can increase alpha brain wave activity, which is associated with a relaxed but focused state of mind (Bhargav et al., 2013). In summary, scientific literature and research suggest that alternate nostril breathing can have psychological and neurological benefits that can improve mental health by reducing stress and anxiety, improving mood, regulating the body's stress response system, and increasing cognitive function.

Here's how to do Alternate Nostril Breathing effectively:

a. Find a quiet and comfortable place to sit in a cross-legged position or on a chair with your feet flat on the ground.

b. Rest your left hand on your left knee with your palm facing up, and bring your right hand to your nose.

c. Use your right thumb to close your right nostril, and inhale deeply through your left nostril.

d. At the top of your inhalation, use your right ring finger to close your left nostril, and exhale slowly and completely through your right nostril.

e. Inhale deeply through your right nostril.

f. At the top of your inhalation, use your right thumb to close your right nostril, and exhale slowly and completely through your left nostril.

g. Repeat this process for several minutes, alternating your breath through each nostril.

h. Focus on your breath and clear your mind of other thoughts as you practice.

5. 4-6-8 Breathing: This technique involves inhaling deeply through your nose for a count of four, holding your breath for a count of six, and exhaling through your mouth for a count of eight. This pattern can be repeated for several minutes to promote relaxation and reduce stress. 4-6-8 breathing is a breathing technique that involves inhaling for 4 seconds, holding the breath for 6 seconds, and exhaling for 8 seconds. This technique can have psychological and neurological benefits that can improve mental health.

Psychologically, 4-6-8 breathing can help to reduce stress and anxiety, as well as improve mood and relaxation. One study found that practicing this technique can reduce symptoms of anxiety and improve relaxation in healthy adults (Ma et al., 2017). Another study found that it can improve mood and reduce stress in patients with anxiety disorders (Ying et al., 2015).

Neurologically, 4-6-8 breathing can help to regulate the autonomic nervous system and the hypothalamic-pituitary-adrenal (HPA) axis, which is the body's stress response system. One study found that practicing this technique can decrease sympathetic nervous system activity and increase parasympathetic nervous system activity, leading to reduced heart rate and blood pressure (Kovacs et al., 2019). Another study found that it can decrease cortisol levels, a stress hormone that can lead to negative effects on mental health (Ma et al., 2017). 4-6-8 breathing can also increase the flow of oxygen to the brain, which can improve cognitive function and overall mental clarity. One study found that it can increase alpha brain wave activity, which is associated with a relaxed but focused state of mind (Jerath et al., 2012).

In summary, scientific literature and research suggest that 4-6-8 breathing can have psychological and neurological benefits that can improve mental health by reducing stress and anxiety, improving mood and relaxation, regulating the body's stress response system, and increasing cognitive function. Here's how to do 4-6-8 breathing effectively:

a. Find a quiet and comfortable place to sit or lie down.

b. Breathe in through your nose for 4 seconds, counting "1, 2, 3, 4" in your mind.

c. Hold your breath for 6 seconds, counting "1, 2, 3, 4, 5, 6" in your mind.

d. Exhale slowly and completely through your mouth for 8 seconds, counting "1, 2, 3, 4, 5, 6, 7, 8" in your mind.

e. Repeat this process for several minutes, focusing on your breath and clearing your mind of other thoughts.

f. Gradually increase the duration of your 4-6-8 breathing sessions as you become more comfortable with the practice.

6. Increasing Sama Vritti (Incremental Equal Breathing): In this technique, you inhale for a count of four, hold your breath for a count of four, and exhale for a count of four. Then, inhale for a count of five, hold for a count of five, and exhale for a count of five. Repeat this pattern, gradually increasing the count of each breath. Incremental equal breathing, also known as increasing sama vritti, is a breathing technique that involves gradually increasing the length of each inhalation, retention, and exhalation. This technique can have several benefits for mental health.

First, incremental equal breathing can help to reduce stress and anxiety, as well as promote relaxation and calmness. The gradual increase in the length of each breath can help to regulate the nervous system, leading to decreased levels of the stress hormone cortisol and increased activity of the parasympathetic nervous system (Sengupta, 2019). One study found that incremental equal breathing can significantly reduce anxiety and improve psychological well-being in individuals with high levels of stress (Sengupta, 2019). Second, incremental equal breathing can improve cognitive function and mental clarity. The increase in oxygen intake and blood flow to the brain can improve focus, concentration, and overall mental alertness (Kjaer et al., 2002). In addition, the rhythmic nature of the breath can help to synchronize brain waves and improve communication between different regions of the brain (Jerath et al., 2012). Finally, incremental equal breathing can improve overall respiratory health and lung function. The gradual increase in the length of each breath can help to strengthen the lungs and improve their capacity for oxygen intake (Sharma et al., 2019). This can lead to increased feelings of energy and vitality.

In summary, incremental equal breathing can have several benefits for mental health, including reducing stress and anxiety, improving cognitive function, and promoting respiratory health. However, it's important to note that individual experiences may vary and that it's always best to consult with a healthcare provider before starting any new breathing or exercise regimen.

Here's how to do incremental equal breathing effectively:

a. Find a quiet and comfortable place to sit or lie down.

b. Breathe in through your nose for 2 seconds, counting "1, 2" in your mind.

c. Hold your breath for 2 seconds, counting "1, 2" in your mind.

d. Exhale through your nose for 2 seconds, counting "1, 2" in your mind.

e. Repeat this process for several breaths, then gradually increase the duration of each phase of your breath by 1 second, so that your next breath is 3 seconds in, 3 seconds hold, and 3 seconds out.

f. Continue increasing the duration of each phase of your breath until you reach a maximum duration that feels comfortable for you, such as 10 seconds in, 10 seconds hold, and 10 seconds out.

g. Focus on your breath and clear your mind of other thoughts as you practice.

7. Breath Counting: In this technique, you count each breath as you inhale and exhale. For example, you might count "one" as you inhale, "two" as you exhale, "three" as you inhale, and so on. This can help focus your mind and calm your thoughts. Breath counting is a simple mindfulness-based breathing technique that involves counting each breath as it is inhaled and exhaled. This technique can have several benefits for mental health. First, breath counting can help to reduce stress and anxiety. Focusing on the breath can help to calm the mind and bring a sense of peace and relaxation. A study published in the Journal of Clinical Psychology found that practicing breath counting for just 10 minutes a day can significantly reduce symptoms of anxiety and depression in individuals with a history of mood disorders (Hoge et al., 2013).

Second, breath counting can improve concentration and focus. The act of counting each breath requires sustained attention and can help to train the mind to stay present in the moment. This can have a positive impact on cognitive function and overall mental performance (Schmalzl et al., 2014). Finally, breath counting can promote better sleep and overall sleep quality. A study published in the Journal of Sleep Research found that practicing breath counting for 20 minutes before bedtime can significantly improve sleep quality and reduce the time it takes to fall asleep (Harinath et al., 2004). In summary, breath counting is a simple and effective breathing technique that can have several benefits for mental health, including reducing stress and anxiety, improving concentration and focus, and promoting better sleep.

Here's how to do breath counting effectively:

a. Find a quiet and comfortable place to sit or lie down.

b. Close your eyes and take a few deep breaths to relax your body and clear your mind.

c. Start breathing naturally through your nose, and count each inhalation and exhalation as one breath, up to a count of 10.

d. If you lose count or get distracted by other thoughts, simply start over at one.

e. Continue to count your breaths for several minutes, focusing on your breath and clearing your mind of other thoughts.

f. Gradually increase the duration of your breath counting sessions as you become more comfortable with the practice.

Remember, the goal of these breathing exercises is to promote relaxation, reduce stress, and improve mental health. It's important to find the technique or techniques that work best for you, and to practice them regularly. Try incorporating these techniques into your daily routine to help manage stress and improve your mental health.

CHAPTER EIGHT

Art Therapy

A. Definition of Art Therapy

Art therapy is a form of psychotherapy that utilizes the creative process of making art to improve mental health and emotional well-being. This therapy allows individuals to express themselves non-verbally, providing a medium through which emotions can be explored and processed. Art therapy has been shown to have numerous benefits for mental health, including reducing symptoms of anxiety and depression, increasing self-awareness and self-esteem, and providing a sense of relaxation and stress relief. There are several mechanisms through which art therapy can benefit mental health. One mechanism is the concept of "flow," which is a state of deep immersion and absorption in an activity. Engaging in the creative process can induce a state of flow, which has been shown to reduce stress and improve mood (Csikszentmihalyi, 1997). Additionally, the act of creating art can provide a sense of accomplishment and mastery, which can increase self-esteem and confidence.

Research has also demonstrated the effectiveness of art therapy for a variety of mental health conditions. A meta-analysis of 45 studies found that art therapy was effective in reducing symptoms of anxiety and depression in individuals with various mental health conditions (Van Lith et al., 2015). Another study found that art therapy was effective in reducing symptoms of post-traumatic stress disorder (PTSD) in military veterans (Schouten et al., 2015). Additionally, a randomized controlled trial found that art therapy was effective in reducing stress and anxiety in women with breast cancer (Monti et al., 2006). In summary, art therapy is a form of psychotherapy that can benefit mental health by reducing symptoms of anxiety and depression, increasing self-awareness and self-esteem, and providing a sense of relaxation and stress relief. The mechanisms through which art therapy works include inducing a state of flow, providing a sense of accomplishment and mastery, and providing a non-verbal outlet for the expression of emotions.

B. Proven Benefits of Art Therapy

Art therapy is a form of therapy that uses creative expression and the arts to help individuals express themselves, work through emotional and psychological challenges, and develop a deeper understanding of themselves and their experiences. Here are some of the proven benefits of art therapy:

1. Reducing stress and anxiety: Engaging in creative activities such as painting, drawing, or sculpture can help individuals relax, reduce stress, and manage anxiety.

2. Improving mood: Creating art has been shown to boost mood and improve overall well-being.

3. Enhancing self-awareness: Art therapy can help individuals explore and express their emotions, thoughts, and feelings in a safe and supportive environment.

4. Enhancing communication skills: Creating art can help individuals express themselves when words are difficult, which can improve communication skills.

5. Fostering self-esteem: Art therapy can help individuals develop a sense of pride and accomplishment, which can lead to an increase in self-esteem.

6. Reducing symptoms of depression: Art therapy has been shown to reduce symptoms of depression and improve mood.

7. Promoting personal growth: Engaging in art therapy can help individuals explore their identity and develop a greater sense of self-awareness and personal growth.

8. Managing trauma: Art therapy has been used to help individuals who have experienced trauma process and manage their experiences in a safe and supportive environment.

9. Supporting physical healing: Art therapy can be used to support physical healing by reducing stress and anxiety, and providing a positive and creative outlet for expression.

Overall, art therapy can be a valuable and effective form of therapy that offers a range of benefits for individuals of all ages and backgrounds.

C. Techniques for Practicing Art Therapy

There are many different techniques used in art therapy, and the most effective technique will depend on the needs of the individual and the goals of the therapy. Here are a few examples of art therapy techniques, along with instructions for how to practice them:

1. Mandala Drawing: Mandala is a circular symbol used in many cultures to represent wholeness, harmony, and balance. Drawing mandalas can be a calming and meditative practice, and can be used to reduce stress and anxiety.

Instructions:

Start by drawing a circle in the center of your paper.

Draw a series of concentric circles around the center circle, creating rings of equal width.

Choose colors that feel calming to you and begin filling in the spaces between the circles with shapes and patterns.

Continue filling in the mandala until you have completed the design.

2. Collage: Collage is a technique that involves cutting and pasting different images and materials together to create a new image. Collage can be used to explore themes related to identity, emotions, and memories.

Instructions:

Start by gathering a variety of materials, such as magazines, newspapers, photographs, and fabrics.

Cut out images and patterns that catch your eye, without worrying about how they will all fit together.

Begin arranging the images and patterns on your paper, moving them around until you find a composition that feels balanced and harmonious.

Glue the images and patterns onto the paper, and add any additional details or embellishments.

3. Scribble Drawing: Scribble drawing is a technique that involves making a series of random marks on paper and then turning those marks into a cohesive image. This technique can be used to encourage free expression and creativity.

Instructions:

Start by making a series of random marks on your paper using a pen, pencil, or other drawing tool.

Look at the marks you have made, and see if you can identify any shapes or images within them.

Use these shapes and images as a starting point for your drawing, filling in the details and adding color as you go.

Continue working on your drawing until you feel it is complete.

4. Finger Painting: Finger painting is a technique that involves using your fingers to apply paint to paper. This technique can be used to encourage sensory exploration and can be particularly effective for individuals who have difficulty expressing themselves with words.

Instructions:

Start by squeezing a few colors of paint onto your palette or paper plate.

Dip your fingers into the paint and begin applying it to the paper.

Experiment with different finger strokes and textures, such as swirling, dotting, or dragging your fingers across the paper.

Allow the painting to evolve and develop naturally, without worrying too much about the end result.

5. Clay Sculpting: Clay sculpting involves working with clay to create three-dimensional objects. This technique can be used to encourage sensory exploration and to express emotions and ideas in a tangible way.

Instructions:

Start by selecting a piece of clay and kneading it until it is soft and pliable.

Begin sculpting the clay into a shape or object that feels meaningful to you.

Use your hands or sculpting tools to shape and refine the object, adding details and textures as you go.

Allow the sculpture to dry and harden, and consider how it represents your emotions or experiences.

6. Mask Making: Mask making involves creating a physical mask that represents different aspects of the self or emotions. This technique can be used to explore identity, emotions, and hidden aspects of the self.

Instructions:

Start by selecting a base for your mask, such as a pre-made mask, a paper plate, or a cardboard cutout.

Begin decorating the mask using a variety of materials, such as paint, markers, feathers, beads, or other decorative items.

Consider the different aspects of your identity or emotions that you would like to represent on the mask, and choose materials that reflect those aspects.

When the mask is complete, consider how it represents different parts of your self or emotions.

7. Guided Drawing: Guided drawing involves following a series of prompts or instructions to create a specific image or design. This technique can be used to encourage mindfulness, relaxation, and creative exploration.

Instructions:

Find a guided drawing resource, such as a book, website, or video, that offers prompts or instructions for drawing a specific image or design.

Set aside a designated time and space for the drawing activity.

Follow the prompts or instructions, focusing on the process of drawing rather than the end result.

Take breaks as needed to stretch, rest, or reflect on the drawing process.

8. Art Journaling: Art journaling involves using a notebook or journal to create a combination of written and visual entries. This technique can be used to explore emotions, track personal growth, and express creativity.

Instructions:

Start by selecting a notebook or journal that feels comfortable to you.

Begin filling the pages with a combination of written and visual entries, using any materials or techniques that feel meaningful to you.

Write about your emotions, experiences, and personal growth, and use images, colors, and designs to enhance the entries.

Make time to regularly work on your art journal, allowing it to become a reflection of your inner thoughts and feelings.

CHAPTER NINE

Time Management

A. The Link between Time Management and Mental Health

Time management refers to the practice of allocating time to different tasks and activities in an efficient and effective manner. Good time management skills involve setting priorities, breaking down large tasks into smaller ones, and creating a schedule or plan for completing them. There is a growing body of scientific evidence that suggests that time management can have a positive impact on mental health.

1. Reduces Stress and Anxiety: Poor time management can lead to feelings of overwhelm, stress, and anxiety. By effectively managing time and breaking down tasks into smaller, manageable chunks, individuals can reduce their stress levels and feel more in control. Research shows that effective time management can help individuals cope with stress and reduce anxiety levels (e.g., Blankson et al., 2021).

2. Increases Productivity: Time management skills can improve productivity, which can boost self-esteem and reduce feelings of guilt or shame. By setting achievable goals and breaking down large tasks into smaller ones, individuals can increase their motivation and focus, leading to greater productivity and a sense of accomplishment. Research shows that effective time management skills are associated with increased productivity and job satisfaction (e.g., Demir, 2019).

3. Improves Sleep Quality: Effective time management can help individuals achieve a better work-life balance, leading to better

sleep quality. By setting realistic schedules and avoiding procrastination, individuals can reduce the need to work late into the night and improve their overall sleep habits. Research shows that poor time management is associated with poor sleep quality and increased sleep disturbances (e.g., Kalmbach et al., 2018).

4. Enhances Psychological Well-being: Good time management can help individuals feel more in control of their lives, which can enhance their overall sense of well-being. By prioritizing activities that are important to them and avoiding activities that drain their energy, individuals can feel more fulfilled and satisfied with their lives. Research shows that effective time management is associated with greater life satisfaction and well-being (e.g., Howell et al., 2016).

Overall, good time management skills can have a positive impact on mental health by reducing stress and anxiety, increasing productivity, improving sleep quality, and enhancing overall well-being. By making time management a priority and implementing strategies to improve it, individuals can experience greater control over their lives and a greater sense of fulfillment and happiness.

B. Effective Time Management Strategies

1. Prioritizing Tasks: The mechanism behind prioritizing tasks is that it helps you focus on what's most important and urgent, and therefore use your time more efficiently. When you have a lot of tasks to complete, it can be easy to get overwhelmed and waste time on low-priority tasks. By prioritizing tasks, you can make sure you're using your time in the most effective way possible. Let's say you have a lot of tasks to complete for work, including responding to emails, preparing a report, and attending a meeting. By prioritizing tasks, you might decide that responding to urgent emails should be done first, followed by preparing the report, and attending the meeting last.

2. Breaking Down Large Tasks: The mechanism behind breaking down large tasks is that it makes the task more manageable and

less overwhelming. When faced with a large task, it's easy to feel paralyzed and not know where to start. By breaking it down into smaller tasks, you can tackle each task one at a time and build momentum as you go. Let's say you have a large project due in a month. By breaking down the project into smaller tasks, you might create a timeline that includes tasks like researching the topic, outlining the project, drafting each section, revising and editing, and finalizing the project.

3. Setting Realistic Goals: The mechanism behind setting realistic goals is that it helps you avoid overcommitting and feeling overwhelmed. When you set goals that are too ambitious or unrealistic, it's easy to feel like you're not making progress and get discouraged. By setting goals that are achievable, you can build momentum and feel a sense of accomplishment as you make progress. Let's say you want to learn a new language, but you don't have much time to devote to it. By setting realistic goals, you might decide to learn a few words and phrases each week, rather than trying to become fluent in a short amount of time.

4. Creating a Schedule: The mechanism behind creating a schedule is that it helps you manage your time more effectively and avoid wasting time on non-essential tasks. When you have a schedule, you know what you need to be doing and when, and therefore you can use your time more efficiently. A schedule can also help you avoid procrastination and stay on track. Let's say you're a student with classes, assignments, and extracurricular activities. By creating a schedule, you might allocate specific blocks of time for each activity, such as attending classes in the morning, studying in the afternoon, and participating in extracurricular activities in the evening.

5. Avoiding Multitasking: The mechanism behind avoiding multitasking is that it helps you stay focused and avoid distractions. When you try to do too many things at once, you can end up feeling overwhelmed and not making progress on any of the tasks. By focusing on one task at a time, you can stay more focused and productive. Let's say you're working on a project and also trying

to respond to emails and messages. By avoiding multitasking, you might focus on the project first, complete it, and then move on to responding to emails and messages.

Overall, by implementing these time management strategies, you can use your time more efficiently and effectively, avoid feeling overwhelmed, and make progress towards your goals, apart from the benefits it has for mental health which we discussed earlier.

C. Tips for Incorporating Time Management into Daily Life

Here are some tips for incorporating these time management strategies into your daily life:

1. Prioritizing Tasks:

- Start your day by making a to-do list of tasks you need to complete.
- Rank the tasks in order of importance and urgency.
- Begin with the highest priority tasks and work your way down the list.
- If you're not sure which tasks are the highest priority, ask your manager or supervisor for guidance.

2. Breaking Down Large Tasks:

- Start by identifying a large project or task that needs to be completed.
- Break it down into smaller, more manageable tasks that can be completed in a reasonable amount of time.
- Create a timeline or schedule for completing each task.
- Set deadlines for each task and hold yourself accountable to them.

3. Setting Realistic Goals:

- Identify a specific goal that you want to achieve.
- Break the goal down into smaller, more achievable steps.
- Set a realistic timeline for completing each step.
- Celebrate each small accomplishment along the way to keep yourself motivated.

4. Creating a Schedule:

• Start by creating a weekly schedule that includes all of your regular commitments, such as work, school, and personal appointments.

• Allocate specific blocks of time for each activity, including tasks like exercise, meal preparation, and self-care.

• Use a planner or calendar app to help you stay on track.

• Review your schedule regularly and make adjustments as needed.

5. Avoiding Multitasking:

• Focus on one task at a time.

• Minimize distractions by turning off notifications and closing unnecessary tabs or windows on your computer.

• Use tools like the Pomodoro Technique, which involves working on one task for a set amount of time, taking a short break, and then returning to the task.

• Be present and mindful in each task, giving it your full attention.

Overall, the key to incorporating these time management strategies into your daily life is to create a routine that works for you. Experiment with different techniques and find the ones that help you stay focused and productive. Remember to be flexible and make adjustments as needed. With practice, you can become more efficient with your time and achieve your goals more effectively.

CHAPTER TEN

Sleep

A. The Importance of Sleep for Mental Health

Sleep is a complex physiological process that is essential for our overall health and well-being, and has a profound impact on our mental health. The relationship between sleep and mental health is complex, and involves a variety of psychological and biological mechanisms. On a psychological level, sleep plays a crucial role in regulating our emotions and mood. Studies have shown that lack of sleep can lead to increased irritability, anxiety, and depressed mood, while getting adequate sleep can improve mood and emotional regulation. This is because during sleep, the brain has the opportunity to consolidate and process emotions and experiences, allowing us to wake up feeling refreshed and with a more balanced perspective on life. Sleep also supports cognitive function, including memory, attention, and decision-making abilities, which can significantly impact our mental health.

On a biological level, sleep is essential for the proper functioning of multiple systems in the body, including the immune, endocrine, and nervous systems. During sleep, the body produces cytokines, which are proteins that help fight off infection, inflammation, and stress. Lack of sleep can impair the immune system's ability to produce cytokines, leading to an increased risk of infection and illness. Sleep also plays a crucial role in regulating the body's stress response, with research showing that chronic sleep deprivation can lead to increased levels of stress hormones like cortisol, which can increase the risk of developing mental health disorders. Another important biological mechanism behind the importance of sleep for mental health is its impact on neural plasticity, which is the brain's ability to adapt and change in response to experience. During sleep, the brain has the opportunity to consolidate and strengthen neural connections, which are essential for learning, memory, and cognitive function. Lack of sleep can impair neural plasticity, leading to cognitive deficits and an increased risk of developing mental health disorders. In addition to psychological and biological mechanisms, sleep also has profound neurological benefits that can impact mental health. During sleep, the brain undergoes important processes, such as the consolidation of memories and the clearance of waste products. Research has found that lack of sleep can lead to impairments in memory consolidation, which can affect learning and cognitive function, and increase the risk of developing mental health disorders. Moreover, sleep is crucial for the clearance of waste products in the brain, such as beta-amyloid, which is a protein that has been linked to the development of Alzheimer's disease. Studies have found that during sleep, the brain's glymphatic system, which is responsible for the clearance of waste products, is more active than during wakefulness. Thus, adequate sleep is essential for maintaining healthy brain function and reducing the risk of developing neurodegenerative disorders.

Additionally, sleep plays a critical role in regulating brain activity, with research indicating that it can influence the activity of the prefrontal cortex, which is the part of the brain responsible for decision-making, attention, and emotional regulation. Studies have found that lack of sleep can lead to impairments in prefrontal cortex function, which can affect mental health outcomes, including an increased risk of developing mood disorders and anxiety. In summary, sleep is essential for maintaining optimal mental health and well-being, and its importance cannot be overstated. Adequate sleep is crucial for regulating emotions, cognitive function, immune function, stress response, neural plasticity, and brain activity, all of which can have significant impacts on mental health outcomes. Ensuring that we get sufficient and high-quality sleep should be a priority for anyone seeking to maintain or improve their mental health.

B. Tips for Improving Sleep

Here are a dozen tips to improve your sleep:

1. Stick to a consistent sleep schedule: Your body's internal clock, or circadian rhythm, operates on a 24-hour cycle and regulates when you feel awake or sleepy. Going to bed and waking up at the same time every day, even on weekends, helps to maintain this natural cycle. This consistency helps your body learn when to expect sleep and wakefulness, making it easier to fall asleep and stay asleep.

2. Create a relaxing bedtime routine: Establishing a relaxing pre-sleep routine can help signal to your body that it's time to wind down and prepare for sleep. This can include activities like taking a warm bath, reading a book, or practicing relaxation techniques like deep breathing. By making relaxation a regular part of your bedtime routine, you can help to reduce stress and anxiety, both of which can interfere with sleep.

3. Make sure your bedroom is conducive to sleep: A comfortable sleep environment can play a big role in getting a good night's sleep. Keep your bedroom cool, quiet, and dark, and invest in comfortable bedding and a supportive mattress. If outside noise is an issue, consider using earplugs or a white noise machine to help mask the sound.

4. Limit exposure to screens before bedtime: The blue light emitted by electronic devices like smartphones, tablets, and computers can interfere with the production of the sleep-inducing hormone melatonin. This can make it harder to fall asleep and lead to more disrupted sleep throughout the night. To minimize the impact of blue light on your sleep, try to avoid using electronic devices for at least an hour before bedtime.

5. Avoid consuming caffeine and alcohol before bedtime: Caffeine is a stimulant that can interfere with sleep quality and

make it harder to fall asleep. To avoid the stimulating effects of caffeine, try to avoid consuming coffee, tea, chocolate, and other caffeinated foods and drinks for several hours before bedtime. Similarly, while alcohol can make you feel drowsy, it can disrupt your natural sleep cycle and lead to more disrupted sleep throughout the night.

6. Exercise regularly: Regular exercise can help to improve sleep quality and help you fall asleep more easily. Exercise can help to reduce stress and anxiety, both of which can interfere with sleep. However, it's important to avoid vigorous activity close to bedtime, as this can have a stimulating effect and make it harder to fall asleep.

7. Don't eat a large meal before bedtime: Eating a large meal before bedtime can interfere with digestion and lead to discomfort, making it harder to fall asleep. To avoid this, try to eat your last meal several hours before bedtime, and if you need a snack, try something light and easy to digest.

8. Reduce stress: Stress and anxiety can interfere with sleep quality and make it harder to fall asleep. Try to manage stress through relaxation techniques like yoga, meditation, or deep breathing exercises. You might also find it helpful to keep a journal or engage in other creative activities that help you unwind and process your thoughts and feelings.

9. Avoid napping during the day: While napping can be a good way to catch up on missed sleep, it can also interfere with your natural sleep cycle and make it harder to fall asleep at night. If you must nap, limit it to 20-30 minutes and avoid napping late in the day.

10. Use your bed for sleep and sex only: Your brain is a powerful associator, and it can learn to associate your bed with activities other than sleep, such as work or watching TV. By reserving your bed for sleep and sex only, you can help to train your brain to associate your bed with sleep. This can make it easier to fall asleep and stay asleep.

CHAPTER ELEVEN

Muscle Relaxation Techniques

A. Progressive Muscle Relaxation

Progressive Muscle Relaxation (PMR) is a relaxation technique that involves tensing and relaxing muscle groups in a systematic way to promote physical and mental relaxation. The technique is based on the idea that when the body is physically relaxed, the mind also tends to become more relaxed, reducing stress and anxiety. The technique involves tensing and then relaxing each muscle group in the body, one at a time. The muscle groups are usually worked on in a specific order, starting from the feet and moving up to the head. During the tensing phase, the muscles are contracted and held for a few seconds, and during the relaxation phase, the muscles are released and allowed to relax completely. The process is repeated for each muscle group, with the aim of gradually reducing tension throughout the body.

The benefits of PMR for mental health are numerous. Here are a few:

1. Reducing stress and anxiety: PMR has been shown to reduce feelings of stress and anxiety by promoting physical relaxation. When the body is relaxed, it sends a signal to the brain that it is safe, reducing the production of stress hormones like cortisol and promoting a sense of calm.

2. Improving sleep: PMR can help improve the quality of sleep by reducing muscle tension and promoting relaxation. Individuals

who practice PMR before bed may find it easier to fall asleep and stay asleep throughout the night.

3. Managing chronic pain: PMR can be effective in managing chronic pain by reducing muscle tension and promoting relaxation. The technique can help individuals with conditions like arthritis or fibromyalgia manage their pain by reducing tension in the muscles surrounding the affected area.

4. Enhancing mindfulness: PMR requires individuals to focus on the physical sensations in their body, which can help promote mindfulness and awareness of the present moment. This can be particularly beneficial for individuals with anxiety or depression, who may benefit from learning to focus on the present moment rather than ruminating on negative thoughts.

5. Boosting mood: PMR has been shown to improve mood and reduce symptoms of depression by promoting physical relaxation and reducing stress. Individuals who practice PMR regularly may find that they feel more calm and positive throughout the day.

Here is a step-by-step guide to practicing Progressive Muscle Relaxation (PMR):

1. Find a quiet, comfortable place where you can lie down or sit in a comfortable chair without being disturbed.

2. Take a few deep breaths and try to clear your mind of any distracting thoughts. Focus your attention on your breathing, and try to slow it down by taking slow, deep breaths in through your nose and out through your mouth.

3. Starting with your toes, tense the muscles in your feet by curling your toes downward, and hold for a few seconds before relaxing completely. Notice the difference in sensation between tension and relaxation. Pay attention to how your muscles feel when they are tensed, and when they are relaxed.

4. Continue working your way up your body, tensing and then relaxing each muscle group. Move on to your calves by pointing your toes upward and tensing your calf muscles, then relaxing them

completely. Next, move on to your thighs by tensing your thigh muscles and then relaxing them completely.

5. Move on to your hips by tensing your gluteal muscles and then relaxing them completely. Then, move on to your abdomen by tightening your abdominal muscles as if you were preparing to do a sit-up, and then relaxing them completely.

6. Continue up your body to your chest by taking a deep breath and holding it for a few seconds, then releasing it completely. Then, move on to your arms by making fists and tensing your biceps, then relaxing completely.

7. Move on to your hands by making fists and clenching your hands, then relaxing completely. Then, move on to your neck by tensing your neck muscles by pressing your chin to your chest, then relaxing completely.

8. Finally, move on to your face by scrunching your eyes tightly shut, then relaxing completely. Then, scrunch your face up as if you were trying to touch your nose to your forehead, then relax completely.

9. Once you have finished tensing and relaxing each muscle group, take a few deep breaths and focus your attention on how your body feels. Notice the sensation of relaxation in your muscles and how your body feels more relaxed overall.

10. Try to practice PMR for 10-15 minutes each day, or whenever you feel stressed or anxious. With regular practice, you will become more skilled at noticing when your muscles are tense, and be able to release that tension more easily. Over time, this can help to reduce stress and promote relaxation and overall mental wellbeing.

B. Passive Muscle Relaxation

Another form of progressive muscle relaxation that can be useful is called "passive muscle relaxation." In passive muscle relaxation, instead of tensing and relaxing each muscle group, you simply focus on relaxing each muscle group without tensing them first.

Here is a step-by-step guide to practicing passive muscle relaxation:

1. Find a quiet, comfortable place where you can lie down or sit in a comfortable chair without being disturbed.

2. Take a few deep breaths and try to clear your mind of any distracting thoughts. Focus your attention on your breathing, and try to slow it down by taking slow, deep breaths in through your nose and out through your mouth.

3. Starting with your toes, focus your attention on relaxing the muscles in your feet. Imagine the tension in your feet melting away as you release all muscle tension.

4. Continue working your way up your body, focusing on relaxing each muscle group. Move on to your calves, then your thighs, hips, abdomen, chest, arms, hands, neck, and face.

5. As you focus on each muscle group, imagine the tension melting away and a feeling of relaxation spreading through your body.

6. Once you have finished relaxing each muscle group, take a few deep breaths and focus your attention on how your body feels. Notice the sensation of relaxation in your muscles and how your body feels more relaxed overall.

7. Try to practice passive muscle relaxation for 10-15 minutes each day, or whenever you feel stressed or anxious. With regular practice, you will become more skilled at noticing when your muscles are tense, and be able to release that tension more easily. Over time, this can help to reduce stress and promote relaxation and overall mental wellbeing.

Both progressive and passive muscle relaxation techniques can be helpful in promoting relaxation and reducing stress and anxiety. It's worth experimenting with both methods to see which one works best for you. Passive Muscle Relaxation has the same benefits as explained for Progressive Muscle Relaxation.

CHAPTER TWELVE

Self-Care

Self-care refers to any intentional actions that an individual takes to care for their physical, mental, and emotional health. It involves making choices that promote overall well-being, and can include things like exercise, healthy eating, stress reduction techniques, and engaging in enjoyable activities.

The scientific basis for self-care lies in the concept of biopsychosocial health, which recognizes that health is influenced by biological, psychological, and social factors. Self-care practices can help improve health in each of these domains. For example:

Biological health: Self-care practices such as exercise, healthy eating, and getting enough sleep can help improve physical health by reducing the risk of chronic diseases and promoting overall well-being. You can support your biological health by these following methods :

- Regular exercise: Exercise has numerous physical health benefits, including reducing the risk of chronic diseases, improving cardiovascular health, and promoting healthy weight management.
- Eating a healthy diet: A diet rich in fruits, vegetables, whole grains, lean proteins, and healthy fats can help reduce the risk of chronic diseases and improve overall health.
- Getting enough sleep: Sleep is important for physical health, and getting enough sleep can improve mood, cognitive function, and overall well-being.
- Drinking enough water: Staying hydrated is important for physical health, and drinking enough water can improve energy

levels and help the body function properly.

- Practicing good hygiene: Good hygiene practices, such as regularly washing hands and taking showers, can help reduce the risk of illness and promote overall physical health.
- Taking breaks throughout the day: Taking short breaks throughout the day can help reduce fatigue and improve mental and physical energy.
- Spending time in nature: Spending time outdoors can help reduce stress and promote physical activity, both of which can improve overall health.
- Getting regular check-ups: Regular doctor and dentist visits can help prevent or catch health issues early, improving overall physical health.
- Avoiding smoking and drug use: These habits can have negative effects on physical health and should be avoided.
- Reducing alcohol consumption: Excessive alcohol consumption can have negative effects on physical health, and reducing alcohol intake can improve overall well-being.
- Using protective equipment: Using protective equipment such as sunscreen, helmets, and seatbelts can help prevent injury and promote physical health.
- Taking prescribed medication: Taking prescribed medication as directed can help manage chronic conditions and improve overall physical health.

Psychological health: Self-care practices such as meditation, relaxation techniques, and engaging in enjoyable activities can help reduce stress and improve mental health. You can support your psychological health by these following methods :

- Mindfulness meditation: Meditation can help reduce stress and anxiety, and promote feelings of calm and relaxation.
- Creative expression: Engaging in creative activities, such as drawing, painting, or writing, can promote relaxation and improve mental health.

- Positive self-programming: Practicing positive self-programming can help improve self-esteem and reduce negative thoughts and feelings.
- Therapy or counseling: Speaking with a mental health professional can help improve mental health by providing tools and techniques to manage stress, anxiety, and other mental health conditions.
- Journaling: Writing down thoughts and feelings can help reduce stress and improve mental health.
- Practicing gratitude: Focusing on the positive aspects of life can help improve mood and promote feelings of happiness and contentment.
- Setting realistic goals: Setting and achieving goals can promote a sense of accomplishment and improve self-esteem.
- Learning new skills: Learning new skills can promote mental stimulation and improve overall cognitive function.
- Engaging in hobbies: Engaging in hobbies can promote relaxation and improve mental health.
- Setting aside time for relaxation: Setting aside time for relaxation, such as taking a warm bath or reading a book, can help reduce stress and improve mental health.
- Getting regular therapy or counseling: Speaking with a mental health professional can help individuals manage mental health conditions and improve overall well-being.
- Practicing self-compassion: Treating oneself with kindness and understanding can promote self-esteem and improve mental health.

<u>Social health</u>: Self-care practices such as connecting with others, participating in social activities, and setting healthy boundaries can help improve social health and reduce feelings of isolation. You can support your social health by these following methods :

- Spending time with loved ones: Maintaining healthy relationships and social connections can help improve overall well-being.

- Volunteering: Volunteering can help improve social health by providing a sense of purpose and connection with others.
- Setting boundaries: Setting boundaries with others can help reduce stress and improve mental health by allowing individuals to prioritize their own needs.
- Joining a social group or club: Joining a group or club that aligns with personal interests can help improve social health by providing opportunities for social connection and engagement.
- Attending social events: Attending social events can help individuals form connections and improve social health.
- Practicing active listening: Practicing active listening skills can help improve communication and promote healthy relationships.
- Participating in group activities: Participating in group activities, such as sports or book clubs, can help improve social health by providing opportunities for social connection.
- Practicing forgiveness: Practicing forgiveness can promote healthy relationships and improve overall well-being.
- Helping others: Helping others, such as volunteering or performing random acts of kindness, can promote a sense of purpose and improve social health.
- Saying "no" when necessary: Saying "no" to requests that may cause undue stress or anxiety can help improve overall well-being by prioritizing individual needs.
- Building a support system: Building a support system of trusted friends and family can improve overall social health by providing a sense of community and support.
- Seeking out new social experiences: Trying new social experiences can help expand social connections and improve overall social health.

Research has also shown that self-care practices can have a positive impact on the body's stress response. Chronic stress can have negative effects on physical and mental health, and self-care practices can help reduce stress levels by activating the body's relaxation response. This response can lower heart rate and blood pressure, reduce muscle tension, and promote feelings of calm and well-being.

Some other dimensions of self-care include :

<u>Emotional self-care:</u>

- Identifying and expressing emotions: Recognizing and expressing emotions can help individuals better understand and manage their emotional state.
- Setting healthy emotional boundaries: Setting limits with others can help individuals maintain emotional well-being and prevent burnout.
- Allowing for self-expression: Engaging in creative activities, such as painting or writing, can promote emotional expression and improve overall emotional health.
- Practicing mindfulness: Practicing mindfulness techniques, such as meditation or deep breathing, can help individuals manage stress and improve emotional well-being.
- Seeking out positive relationships: Seeking out relationships with people who uplift and support can improve emotional health.

<u>Spiritual self-care:</u>

- Engaging in spiritual practices: Engaging in practices such as prayer, meditation, or attending religious services can promote a sense of purpose and improve overall spiritual health.
- Connecting with nature: Spending time in nature can help individuals feel more connected to the world around them and improve overall spiritual health.
- Seeking out meaningful experiences: Seeking out experiences that feel meaningful and fulfilling, such as volunteering or engaging in creative activities, can promote overall spiritual health.

• Reflecting on personal values: Reflecting on personal values can help individuals better understand their beliefs and improve overall spiritual well-being.

• Embracing gratitude: Focusing on feelings of gratitude can promote a sense of well-being and improve overall spiritual health.

Professional self-care:

• Setting professional boundaries: Setting limits around work hours and responsibilities can help individuals prevent burnout and improve overall professional well-being.

• Seeking professional development opportunities: Seeking out opportunities to learn new skills or take on new challenges can help individuals feel fulfilled and improve overall professional growth.

• Taking breaks throughout the workday: Taking short breaks throughout the workday can help reduce stress and improve overall productivity and well-being.

• Seeking feedback and support: Seeking feedback from supervisors and support from colleagues can help individuals improve performance and overall professional well-being.

• Practicing time management: Managing time effectively can help individuals feel more in control of their workload and improve overall professional well-being.

Financial self-care:

• Setting and sticking to a budget: Managing finances effectively can help individuals reduce stress and improve overall financial well-being.

• Saving and investing wisely: Planning for the future and making smart financial decisions can promote a sense of security and improve overall financial health.

• Seeking financial advice when needed: Consulting with a financial advisor or other professional can help individuals make informed financial decisions and improve overall financial well-being.

Physical self-care:

• Eating a balanced and nutritious diet: Eating healthy foods can help individuals maintain physical health and prevent disease.

• Exercising regularly: Regular physical activity can improve physical health, reduce stress, and promote overall well-being.

• Getting enough sleep: Getting enough sleep is essential for physical and mental health and can improve overall well-being.

• Practicing good hygiene: Practicing good hygiene, such as washing hands and brushing teeth, can prevent illness and improve overall physical health.

• Seeking medical care when needed: Seeking medical attention when experiencing symptoms or illness can help individuals maintain physical health and prevent serious health issues.

Intellectual self-care:

• Reading or learning new things: Engaging in activities that promote intellectual growth and learning can promote overall well-being.

• Pursuing hobbies or interests: Engaging in activities that bring joy and fulfillment can promote overall intellectual and emotional health.

• Setting personal goals: Setting and working toward personal goals can promote a sense of purpose and improve overall intellectual and emotional well-being.

• Seeking out challenges: Taking on challenges and pushing oneself outside of one's comfort zone can promote growth and improve overall intellectual and emotional well-being.

• Disconnecting from technology: Taking breaks from technology and engaging in activities that require focus and concentration can improve overall intellectual well-being.

Overall, self-care is an important aspect of maintaining good health and well-being. While there is no one-size-fits-all approach to self-care, finding practices that work for you can help improve physical, mental, and emotional health.

CHAPTER THIRTEEN

Self-Improvement

Working on self-improvement can significantly support mental health and function as an immune system for the mind. By enhancing self-awareness, building self-esteem and self-confidence, promoting self-acceptance, increasing self-motivation and self-direction, and improving self-image and self-identity, individuals can experience numerous benefits for their mental health. Developing greater self-awareness can lead to better emotional regulation, reducing symptoms of anxiety and depression. Improving self-esteem and self-confidence can provide a sense of accomplishment and increase confidence in oneself, leading to a more positive outlook on life. Promoting self-acceptance can help individuals better manage their self-criticism, leading to improved mental health. Increasing self-motivation and self-direction can provide a sense of purpose and direction, which can help reduce feelings of boredom and stagnation, contributing to depression and anxiety. Improving self-image and self-identity can lead to a stronger sense of self and a better understanding of personal values and goals, ultimately increasing resilience and promoting mental well-being.

Self-improvement is the process of actively working towards improving oneself in various areas of life, such as physical health, emotional well-being, relationships, and professional success. It includes a variety of aspects, such as self-identity, self-esteem, self-confidence, self-awareness, self-acceptance, self-direction, self-motivation, self-respect, self-worth, self-image, and self-identity.

Each of these aspects is interconnected and influences one's overall well-being. For example, having a strong sense of self-esteem and self-confidence can lead to greater resilience and the ability to bounce back from setbacks. Self-awareness can help individuals recognize their strengths and weaknesses, which can aid in personal growth and development. Self-acceptance and self-respect are crucial for developing healthy relationships with oneself and others. Self-direction and self-motivation are necessary for setting and achieving goals, while self-worth and self-image impact one's overall sense of satisfaction with life.

By focusing on each of these aspects and actively working to improve them, individuals can increase their sense of self-worth, build a more positive self-image, and improve their overall well-being. The steps for improving each of these aspects are unique, but they all involve a combination of self-reflection, setting achievable goals, and taking action towards positive change. By prioritizing self-improvement and working to strengthen these different aspects of self-identity, individuals can cultivate a greater sense of purpose, fulfillment, and happiness in their lives.

Self-esteem:

1. Practice self-care, such as getting enough sleep, exercising, and eating well.
2. Take time to do things you enjoy and that make you feel good.
3. Surround yourself with positive and supportive people.
4. Challenge negative self-programming and practice positive affirmations.
5. Practice forgiveness towards yourself and others.
6. Set achievable goals and celebrate progress.
7. Focus on your strengths and achievements.
8. Keep a journal to track your progress and reflect on your experiences.

Self-confidence:

1. Identify your strengths and areas for improvement.
2. Practice self-compassion and challenge negative self-programming.
3. Take on new challenges and set achievable goals.
4. Learn new skills and build your knowledge.
5. Surround yourself with positive and supportive people.
6. Practice positive visualization and self-affirmations.
7. Celebrate your successes and take pride in your accomplishments.
8. Learn to accept and learn from failures and setbacks.

Self-awareness:

1. Practice mindfulness and reflection to identify your thoughts, emotions, and behaviors.
2. Identify your personal values and beliefs.
3. Explore your interests and passions.
4. Practice empathy towards yourself and others.
5. Identify your strengths and weaknesses.
6. Learn to accept feedback and criticism.
7. Seek out new experiences and challenges.
8. Take time to reflect on your experiences and personal growth.

Self-acceptance:

1. Practice self-compassion and challenge negative self-programming.
2. Learn to accept and embrace your flaws and imperfections.
3. Focus on the present moment and practice mindfulness.

4. Practice forgiveness towards yourself and others.
5. Identify and challenge any limiting beliefs about yourself.
6. Surround yourself with positive and supportive people.
7. Set realistic expectations for yourself.
8. Embrace your unique qualities and embrace your individuality.

Self-direction:

1. Set clear and achievable goals for yourself.
2. Develop a plan of action to achieve your goals.
3. Practice time management and prioritize tasks.
4. Take initiative and be proactive in achieving your goals.
5. Seek out new experiences and challenges.
6. Build your skills and knowledge through learning and practice.
7. Stay motivated and focused on your goals.
8. Practice self-reflection to ensure you are on the right path.

Self-motivation:

1. Identify your personal values and goals.
2. Set clear and achievable goals for yourself.
3. Build momentum by breaking down larger goals into smaller achievable tasks.
4. Celebrate your successes and take pride in your accomplishments.
5. Practice positive self-programming and affirmations.
6. Find inspiration and motivation in your passions and interests.
7. Surround yourself with positive and supportive people.
8. Stay focused and determined in the face of setbacks and challenges.

Self-respect:

1. Identify and set boundaries for yourself.
2. Speak up for yourself and your needs.
3. Treat yourself with kindness and compassion.
4. Practice assertiveness and confidence.
5. Surround yourself with positive and supportive people.
6. Take care of yourself physically and mentally.
7. Learn to accept and embrace your flaws and imperfections.
8. Practice forgiveness towards yourself and others.

Self-worth:

1. Focus on your positive qualities and strengths.
2. Celebrate your successes and take pride in your accomplishments.
3. Practice self-care and take care of your physical and mental health.
4. Surround yourself with positive and supportive people.
5. Challenge negative self-programming and practice positive affirmations.
6. Practice forgiveness towards yourself and others.
7. Identify and challenge any limiting beliefs about yourself.
8. Practice gratitude and appreciate the positive things in your life.

Self-image:

1. Engage in activities that bring you joy and make you feel fulfilled.

2. Set goals for yourself and work towards achieving them.
3. Take time to rest and recharge when you need it.
4. Spend time with people who make you feel good about yourself.
5. Celebrate your accomplishments, no matter how small they may seem.
6. Engage in self-care practices that make you feel good, such as taking a relaxing bath, getting a massage, or doing yoga.
7. Practice self-compassion and forgive yourself for mistakes or shortcomings.
8. Focus on your strengths and accomplishments, rather than your shortcomings or failures.

<u>Self-Care:</u>

1. Make time for yourself each day to relax and recharge.
2. Take care of your physical health by eating well, exercising regularly, and getting enough sleep.
3. Engage in activities that bring you joy and make you feel good.
4. Practice mindfulness and meditation to reduce stress and improve well-being.
5. Set boundaries to protect your time and energy.
6. Learn to say "no" when necessary and prioritize your own needs.
7. Spend time in nature and get outside to improve your mood and reduce stress.
8. Take care of your emotional health by seeking support when you need it and engaging in activities that promote happiness and fulfillment.

<u>Self-discipline</u> is also an essential aspect of personal growth and self-improvement. It refers to the ability to control your thoughts, emotions, and behaviors in pursuit of your goals, even when faced with distractions, temptations, or obstacles. Developing self-discipline takes time and effort, but it can help you achieve greater success, improve your overall well-being, and build positive habits and routines in your life.

Here are a dozen practical methods that you can do by yourself to build self-discipline:.

1. Set clear goals: Take the time to identify what you want to achieve in the long term. Break these goals down into smaller, achievable steps, and create a timeline for reaching each milestone.
2. Develop a routine: Create a daily routine that includes regular exercise, healthy eating, and productive work. This routine should be personalized to your needs and preferences.
3. Prioritize your tasks: Identify your most important tasks and focus on completing them first. Eliminate distractions, such as social media, during this time.
4. Practice self-control: Learn to resist temptation and delay gratification. This may involve setting limits on certain behaviors, such as limiting your screen time or avoiding unhealthy foods.
5. Track your progress: Keep track of your progress towards your goals. Celebrate small victories along the way, and adjust your plans as needed.
6. Learn from failures: Use failures as an opportunity to learn and improve. Reflect on what went wrong and develop a plan for how to do better next time.
7. Surround yourself with positive influences: Surround yourself with people who support your goals and avoid negative influences. Seek out role models who embody the traits you want to develop.
8. Stay motivated: Find ways to stay motivated, such as rewarding yourself for achieving milestones or seeking support from others. Use positive self-programming and visualization to stay focused on your goals.

9. Practice mindfulness: Learn to be present in the moment and focus your attention on your goals. This may involve meditation or other mindfulness practices.
10. Build self-awareness: Be aware of your thoughts, emotions, and behaviors. Use journaling or self-reflection to gain a deeper understanding of yourself.
11. Practice visualization: Visualize yourself achieving your goals. Focus on the positive outcomes and use this visualization to stay motivated.
12. Be consistent: Practice self-discipline consistently, even when it's challenging. This will help you build positive habits and routines over time. Start small and work your way up, celebrating each small success along the way.

Part Two

Guidance for Mental Health Disorders

CHAPTER FOURTEEN

Anxiety disorders

These are a group of disorders that involve excessive fear, worry, and apprehension, such as generalized anxiety disorder, panic disorder, and phobias. It also includes OCD (Obsessive-Compulsive Disorder.) While there is no single trick that can instantly heal anxiety, there are some practical methods that can help reduce anxiety in the moment. Here are a dozen practical tricks to try:

1. Take deep breaths: When you feel anxious, find a quiet place to sit or stand. Take a slow, deep breath in through your nose for 4-5 seconds. Hold the breath for a few seconds, and then slowly exhale through your mouth for 4-5 seconds. Repeat this for several minutes until you feel more relaxed.

2. Use grounding techniques: Focus on the present moment by using your senses. Name five things you can see, four things you can touch, three things you can hear, two things you can smell, and one thing you can taste. For example, "I see a blue sky, I feel the texture of my shirt, I hear birds chirping, I smell flowers, I taste the mint in my mouth."

3. Use positive self-programming: Repeat positive affirmations to yourself, such as "I am calm" or "I am safe". You can say these to yourself silently or out loud.

4. Visualize a peaceful place: Close your eyes and imagine a place where you feel calm and safe, such as a beach or a forest. Imagine the sights, sounds, and smells of this place.

5. Practice progressive muscle relaxation: Lie down or sit in a comfortable position and focus on your feet. Tense the muscles

in your feet for 5-10 seconds, and then release. Move on to your calves, thighs, stomach, shoulders, arms, and face, tensing and releasing each muscle group. Repeat for a few minutes.

6. Use aromatherapy: Use essential oils, such as lavender or peppermint, to help calm your mind and body. You can put a few drops on a tissue or handkerchief and inhale the scent, or use a diffuser.

7. Listen to calming music: Play music that you find soothing, such as classical music or nature sounds. Focus on the music and allow it to help you relax.

8. Do a quick workout: Exercise releases endorphins, which can help reduce anxiety. Do a quick workout, such as jumping jacks or a few yoga poses, for a few minutes.

9. Use a stress ball: Squeezing a stress ball can help release tension. You can find stress balls online or at a local store.

10. Practice mindfulness: Focus on your breath and the present moment, without judgment or distraction. If your mind wanders, gently bring it back to your breath.

11. Drink herbal tea: Certain teas, such as chamomile or valerian root, have calming properties that can help reduce anxiety. Brew a cup of tea and enjoy it slowly.

12. Seek support: Talk to a friend or family member, or call a helpline, to get support and reassurance. Sharing your thoughts and feelings with someone else can help you feel less alone and more supported.

Desensitization Therapy

Desensitizing and modifying fear, fearful thoughts, and memories is a process that can help you overcome your fears and lead a more fulfilling life. This process involves gradually exposing yourself to the feared situation or thought, so you become desensitized to it and can approach it with less fear and anxiety. Here is a step-by-step guide for desensitizing and modifying fear, along with multiple examples to illustrate the process:

Step 1: Identify the fear

The first step is to identify the fear or situation that causes you distress. It's important to be specific and clear about what exactly you're afraid of. Here are some examples of fears:

Fear of flying

Fear of public speaking

Fear of heights

Fear of spiders

Step 2: Learn about the fear

Once you have identified your fear, the next step is to learn about it. This can help you understand why you are afraid and what triggers your fear response. Here are some ways to learn about your fear:

Research the causes and symptoms of the fear

Talk to a therapist or counselor who specializes in treating your fear

Read books or articles about your fear

For example, if you have a fear of flying, you may research the statistics on airplane safety and learn about the physics of flight. If you have a fear of public speaking, you may research techniques for managing stage fright and improving your speaking skills.

Step 3: Create a fear hierarchy

A fear hierarchy is a list of situations that trigger your fear, ranked from least to most anxiety-provoking. Here are some examples of fear hierarchies:

Fear of flying:

1. Looking at pictures of airplanes
2. Watching videos of takeoff and landing
3. Going to an airport
4. Boarding an airplane

Fear of public speaking:

1. Speaking in front of a small group of friends

2. Speaking in front of a small group of strangers
3. Speaking in front of a larger group of coworkers
4. Giving a presentation to a large audience

Step 4: Exposure therapy

Exposure therapy is a key component of desensitizing and modifying fear. It involves gradually exposing yourself to the situations on your fear hierarchy, starting with the least anxiety-provoking situation and working your way up. Here are some examples of exposure therapy:

Fear of flying:

Start by looking at pictures of airplanes, then move on to watching videos of takeoff and landing. Over time, you may work your way up to going to an airport and boarding an airplane.

Fear of public speaking:

Start by speaking in front of a small group of friends, then move on to speaking in front of strangers and larger groups of coworkers. Over time, you may work your way up to giving a presentation to a large audience.

Step 5: Cognitive restructuring

Cognitive restructuring involves changing your negative thoughts and beliefs about the fear. This can help reduce your anxiety and make it easier to face the fear. Here are some examples of cognitive restructuring:

Fear of flying:

Replace negative thoughts like "I‘m going to crash" with more realistic thoughts like "Air travel is safe, and millions of people fly every day without incident."

Fear of public speaking:

Replace negative thoughts like "I’m going to embarrass myself" with more realistic thoughts like "It’s okay to make mistakes, and everyone does it."

Step 6: Repeat the process

Desensitizing and modifying fear is not a one-time process. It may take time and practice to overcome the fear completely. You may need to repeat the exposure therapy and cognitive restructuring process several times before you feel comfortable in the feared situation.

Self-Questioning Therapy :

Anxiety is a common experience for many people, and it can be challenging to know how to cope with it. One approach is to ask yourself specific questions that can help you identify and address the source of your anxiety. Here are a dozen detailed questions that you can ask yourself to reduce your anxiety:

1. What is causing my anxiety right now?
2. What is the worst that could happen in this situation?
3. What evidence do I have to support my anxious thoughts?
4. Is there any evidence that contradicts my anxious thoughts?
5. How likely is it that my anxious thoughts will come true?
6. What can I do right now to make myself feel more comfortable?
7. Am I catastrophizing the situation?
8. Is my anxiety proportional to the situation at hand?
9. Have I experienced similar situations before, and if so, how did I handle them?
10. What advice would I give a friend who was feeling anxious in this situation?
11. What is the best-case scenario, and how can I work towards that?
12. What steps can I take to prevent this situation from happening again in the future?

To effectively use these questions, take some time to sit down and reflect on the situation that is causing you anxiety. Write down your answers to each of the questions, and be as honest and detailed as possible. Then, take a step back and review your answers to gain some perspective on the situation. Use this information to come up with an action plan that will help you manage your anxiety and work towards a positive outcome. Remember to be kind to yourself and take small steps towards progress.

CHAPTER FIFTEEN

Depressive disorders

This includes major depressive disorder, dysthymia, and bipolar disorder, including others which involve feelings of sadness, hopelessness, and loss of interest in activities. It's important to note that depression is a complex mental health condition that often requires ongoing treatment and management. However, there are some practical methods that can help alleviate symptoms of depression in the moment. Here are a dozen practical tricks to try:

1. Practice deep breathing: Slow, deep breathing can help reduce stress and calm your mind. Take a deep breath in through your nose for 4-5 seconds, hold it for a few seconds, and then exhale slowly through your mouth for 4-5 seconds.

2. Use positive self-programming: Practice speaking to yourself positively and compassionately. This can help reduce negative self-programming and boost your mood.

3. Get moving: Exercise releases endorphins, which can help boost mood and reduce symptoms of depression. Take a walk, go for a run, or do some yoga.

4. Practice mindfulness: Focus on the present moment without judgment. Try meditation, deep breathing, or simply observing your surroundings without judgment.

5. Spend time in nature: Being outside in nature can help improve mood and reduce symptoms of depression. Go for a walk in the park, sit by a river, or simply spend time in your backyard.

6. Connect with others: Social support is important for managing depression. Connect with a friend, family member, or

therapist to talk about your feelings and experiences.

7. Do something creative: Engaging in a creative activity, such as painting, writing, or playing music, can help improve mood and reduce symptoms of depression.

8. Practice gratitude: Make a list of things you're grateful for or write a thank-you note to someone. Focusing on the positive can help shift your mood.

9. Take a break: Take a break from the stressors in your life and do something that you enjoy. Watch a funny movie, take a bubble bath, or read a book.

10. Challenge negative thoughts: When negative thoughts arise, challenge them with evidence and logic. Ask yourself if they are really true or if there is another way to interpret the situation.

11. Get enough sleep: Lack of sleep can worsen depression symptoms. Make sure to get enough sleep each night by practicing good sleep hygiene.

12. Engage in self-care: Take care of yourself by eating nutritious foods, practicing good hygiene, and engaging in activities that make you feel good. Self-care is an important part of managing depression.

Desensitization Therapy

Depression can cause negative thoughts, feelings, and emotions that can be challenging to cope with. Depression can be a debilitating mental health condition that affects many people. One of the symptoms of depression is negative and self-defeating thought patterns, which can lead to a cycle of rumination and low mood. Desensitizing and modifying depressive memories and thought processes is a technique that can help to break this cycle and alleviate some of the symptoms of depression. By using evidence-based counterarguments and re-examining negative thoughts and memories in a more positive and balanced light, individuals can begin to desensitize to their negative effects and cultivate a more positive outlook. Here is a step-by-step guide on how to desensitize and modify depressive memories and thought processes.

1. Find a quiet and comfortable place to sit or lie down. Make sure you will not be interrupted during this process.

2. Use a relaxation technique such as deep breathing, visualization, or progressive muscle relaxation to enter a relaxed and focused state of mind. Deep breathing involves breathing slowly and deeply, focusing on your breath and letting go of any tension in your body. Visualization involves creating a mental image of a calming and peaceful scene. Progressive muscle relaxation involves tensing and releasing the muscles in your body, one group at a time.

3. Once you are in a relaxed and focused state, identify a negative thought or memory that is contributing to your depressive feelings. This could be a recent event or a long-standing pattern of thinking.

4. Hold the negative thought or memory in your mind and examine it objectively. Ask yourself questions such as, "Is this thought or memory based on fact, or is it a distortion?" or "Is there evidence that contradicts this thought or memory?"

5. Challenge the negative thought or memory with evidence-based counterarguments. For example, if the negative thought is, "I am a failure," you could counter it with evidence such as, "I have succeeded in many areas of my life."

6. Re-examine the negative thought or memory with the counterarguments in mind. Try to see the situation in a more positive and balanced light.

7. Repeat this process with any other negative thoughts or memories that are contributing to your depressive feelings.

8. As you work through the negative thoughts and memories, you may notice that they begin to lose their emotional intensity. This is a sign that you are desensitizing to their negative effects.

9. Once you have worked through all of the negative thoughts and memories, take some time to reflect on your experience. Notice any changes in how you feel about the memories or thoughts. You may find that they no longer have the same power over you.

10. Repeat this process as often as needed, with different negative thoughts or memories that come up. Over time, you may find that your overall thought patterns become more positive and balanced, and your depressive symptoms begin to lift.

11. It's important to remember that desensitizing and modifying depressive memories and thought processes is a process that takes time and practice. Be patient with yourself and seek the support of a mental health professional if needed.

Self-Questioning Therapy :

Depression can be a difficult and debilitating experience for many people. While there is no simple solution to overcoming depression, asking yourself specific questions can be a helpful approach to addressing and managing the symptoms. Here are a dozen detailed questions that you can ask yourself to reduce your depression:

1. What am I grateful for in my life right now?
2. What are some things that I've accomplished that I am proud of?
3. What makes me feel happy or content?
4. What small tasks can I complete today that will give me a sense of accomplishment?
5. What can I do to take care of myself right now?
6. What is one thing that I can look forward to in the near future?
7. What is one positive change that I can make in my life?
8. What are some things that I enjoy doing that I haven't done in a while?
9. What is one good thing that happened today?
10. What are some things that I appreciate about myself?
11. What is one thing that I can do to help someone else today?
12. What would I say to a friend who was experiencing depression, and how can I apply that advice to myself?

To use these questions effectively, take some time to sit down and reflect on your current state of mind. Write down your answers to each of the questions, and be as honest and specific as possible. Then, review your answers and try to identify any common themes or patterns. Use this information to come up with an action plan that will help you manage your depression and work towards a more positive outlook. Remember to be kind to yourself and take small steps towards progress, and seek help from a mental health professional if needed.

CHAPTER SIXTEEN

Trauma related disorders

This includes post-traumatic stress disorder (PTSD) and acute stress disorder, which can develop after experiencing or witnessing a traumatic event. Trauma and stress-related disorders, including post-traumatic stress disorder (PTSD) and acute stress disorder, can develop after experiencing or witnessing a traumatic event. Symptoms can include flashbacks, nightmares, hypervigilance, and avoidance of triggers. These symptoms can be distressing and interfere with daily life. While professional help may be necessary for treating these disorders, there are also practical methods that individuals can use to manage symptoms in the moment.

1. Practice deep breathing: Deep breathing can help reduce stress and promote relaxation. Breathe in deeply through your nose for 4-5 seconds, hold it for a few seconds, and then exhale slowly through your mouth for 4-5 seconds. Repeat this process several times.

2. Engage in physical activity: Exercise can help reduce stress and improve mood. Consider going for a walk, doing yoga, or participating in a sport or fitness class.

3. Connect with others: Social support can help alleviate symptoms of trauma and stress-related disorders. Reach out to friends, family, or a therapist for support.

4. Practice grounding techniques: Grounding techniques can help you feel more connected to the present moment. Try focusing on your senses or using a grounding object, such as a favorite stone or piece of jewelry.

5. Write about your experiences: Writing can be a therapeutic way to process trauma and emotions. Try keeping a journal or writing a letter to yourself or someone else.

6. Use positive affirmations: Positive self-programming can help promote self-compassion and resilience. Try using positive affirmations, such as "I am strong" or "I can handle this."

7. Practice relaxation techniques: Relaxation techniques, such as progressive muscle relaxation or guided imagery, can help reduce stress and promote relaxation.

8. Get enough sleep: Sleep is important for physical and mental health. Try to establish a consistent sleep routine and create a relaxing bedtime routine.

9. Limit exposure to triggers: Avoid or limit exposure to triggers, such as certain people or places, that can elicit traumatic memories or emotions.

10. Set boundaries: Establishing healthy boundaries can help you feel more in control of your environment and relationships.

11. Seek professional help: Trauma and stress-related disorders can be complex and may require professional help. Consider seeking the support of a therapist or other mental health professional.

12. Engage in self-care: Practicing self-care, such as eating well, practicing good hygiene, and engaging in activities you enjoy, can help promote overall well-being and reduce stress.

Desensitization Therapy

Desensitization of traumatic memories using self-hypnosis is a technique that can be helpful in managing symptoms of post-traumatic stress disorder (PTSD) and other trauma-related disorders. It's important to note that if you have experienced trauma, it's recommended to work with a qualified mental health professional who can provide guidance and support throughout the process. However, if you're interested in learning how to use self-hypnosis for desensitization of traumatic memories, here's a step-by-step guide:

Step 1: Find a quiet and comfortable place

Find a quiet and comfortable place where you can relax without being disturbed. This could be a room in your home, a park, or any other place where you feel safe and at ease. Ensure that you won't be interrupted during the process. Find a space that is quiet and free from distractions. Sit or lie down comfortably, ensuring that you won't be interrupted during the process. If you're sitting, sit in a chair with your feet flat on the ground, and if you're lying down, lie on a comfortable surface with a pillow to support your head.

Step 2: Induce a state of relaxation

Take a few deep breaths and focus on relaxing your body. You can do this by closing your eyes, visualizing a peaceful scene, or listening to calming music. Allow yourself to fully let go of any tension or stress in your body. You can also use progressive muscle relaxation techniques, where you tense and relax each muscle group in your body, to help you relax further. Take several deep breaths, inhaling slowly through your nose and exhaling through your mouth. As you exhale, imagine all the tension and stress leaving your body. You can also use a visualization technique to help you relax further, such as imagining yourself in a peaceful place, like a beach or a forest.

Step 3: Enter a hypnotic state

When you feel fully relaxed, begin to focus on a specific traumatic memory that you wish to desensitize. While keeping this memory in mind, repeat a calming mantra to yourself, such as "I am safe and in control." This will help you enter a hypnotic state and allow you to more effectively work with the memory. You can also visualize a protective shield around yourself to help you feel safe and secure. Once you are in a state of deep relaxation, focus your attention on a specific traumatic memory that you want to desensitize. Begin to repeat a calming mantra to yourself, such as "I am safe and in control." You can also visualize a protective shield around yourself to help you feel safe and secure. As you continue to focus on the memory, allow yourself to feel a sense of detachment from it, as if you are observing the memory from a distance.

Step 4: Desensitize the memory

Once you're in a hypnotic state, begin to mentally review the traumatic memory from a safe and detached perspective. This means observing the memory as if you were watching a movie or reading a story, rather than reliving the experience. This will help to desensitize the memory and reduce its emotional impact on you. You can also use visualization techniques to modify the memory, such as changing the color of the image or altering the characters' behaviors. As you continue to focus on the memory, try to modify the details of the memory. You can do this by visualizing the memory in a different color or changing the characters' behaviors. You can also try to replace the memory with a positive or neutral experience. For example, if you are recalling a traumatic car accident, you can imagine yourself in a peaceful place, like a garden or a beach. As you do this, focus on your breathing and continue to repeat your calming mantra.

Step 5: Practice self-compassion

Throughout this process, it's important to practice self-compassion and be gentle with yourself. If you feel overwhelmed or distressed at any point, take a break and return to the process later. You can also seek support from a mental health professional or trusted friend or family member. It's important to remember that this process can take time and multiple sessions to be effective, so don't get discouraged if you don't see immediate results. As you work through the process, be kind and gentle with yourself. If you start to feel overwhelmed or distressed, take a break and return to the process later. It's important to remember that this process can take time and multiple sessions to be effective, so don't get discouraged if you don't see immediate results. If you are finding the process challenging, it may be helpful to work with a mental health professional who can guide you through the process.

Overall, self-hypnosis for desensitization of traumatic memories can be a powerful tool in managing PTSD symptoms and other trauma-related disorders. However, it's important to approach this technique with caution and work with a mental health professional if you have any concerns or questions.

Self-Questioning Therapy :

Trauma and stress-related disorders, such as acute stress disorder (ASD) and post-traumatic stress disorder (PTSD), can be challenging experiences for many people. Asking yourself specific questions can be a helpful approach to managing your symptoms and improving your mental health. Here are a dozen detailed questions that you can ask yourself to reduce your trauma and stress-related disorders:

1. What are some specific triggers or situations that make me feel anxious or overwhelmed?
2. What are some coping mechanisms that have worked for me in the past?
3. What physical sensations do I experience when I'm feeling triggered, and how can I address them?
4. What is one thing that I can do to take care of myself right now?
5. What are some healthy ways that I can express my emotions?
6. What are some activities or hobbies that I enjoy that help me relax and feel calm?
7. Who can I reach out to for support when I'm feeling overwhelmed?
8. What are some positive affirmations or statements that I can say to myself when I'm feeling triggered?
9. What are some things that I appreciate about myself and my resilience?
10. What is one small step that I can take towards my goals, despite my symptoms?
11. What is one way that I can practice self-compassion and forgiveness towards myself?
12. What resources or professional help can I seek to address my trauma and stress-related symptoms?

To use these questions effectively, take some time to sit down and reflect on your current symptoms and triggers. Write down your answers to each of the questions, and be as honest and specific as possible. Then, use this information to come up with an action plan that will help you manage your symptoms and work towards a positive outlook. Remember to be kind to yourself and take small steps towards progress, and seek professional help from a mental health provider if needed.

CHAPTER SEVENTEEN

Addictions

This includes addiction to drugs, alcohol, or other substances, which can cause significant impairment in functioning and lead to a range of negative consequences.

Substance abuse disorders and addictions can be challenging to overcome, but there are practical methods that individuals can use to manage symptoms and promote recovery. These methods can be used in conjunction with professional treatment or as standalone strategies.

1. Practice mindfulness: Mindfulness can help you become more aware of your thoughts, emotions, and physical sensations. Try practicing mindfulness meditation or other mindfulness exercises to help manage cravings and stay present in the moment.

2. Connect with support groups: Support groups, such as Alcoholics Anonymous or Narcotics Anonymous, can provide social support and a sense of community. Consider attending meetings or connecting with others in recovery.

3. Set realistic goals: Setting realistic goals can help you stay motivated and focused on your recovery. Start with small goals and gradually work your way up.

4. Create a relapse prevention plan: A relapse prevention plan can help you identify triggers, warning signs, and coping strategies to use in case of a relapse. Consider creating a written plan and sharing it with a trusted friend or family member.

5. Engage in regular exercise: Exercise can help reduce stress, improve mood, and promote overall health. Consider incorporating

regular exercise into your daily routine.

6. Practice self-compassion: Self-compassion can help you develop a more positive attitude towards yourself and your recovery. Practice self-compassion by speaking to yourself in a kind and supportive way.

7. Use distraction techniques: Distraction techniques can help you manage cravings and stay focused on your recovery. Try engaging in a hobby, listening to music, or watching a movie.

8. Avoid triggers: Avoiding triggers, such as certain people or places, can help reduce the likelihood of a relapse. Identify your triggers and make a plan to avoid or minimize them.

9. Seek professional help: Substance abuse disorders and addictions can be complex and may require professional help. Consider seeking the support of a therapist, counselor, or addiction specialist.

10. Practice healthy coping strategies: Healthy coping strategies, such as deep breathing, visualization, and progressive muscle relaxation, can help manage stress and promote relaxation.

11. Establish a support system: A strong support system can provide encouragement, accountability, and social support. Consider reaching out to family, friends, or a sponsor for support.

12. Practice good self-care: Practicing good self-care, such as getting enough sleep, eating a healthy diet, and practicing good hygiene, can help promote overall well-being and reduce stress.

De-addiction plan #1

Drug addiction can be a difficult and challenging condition to overcome, but with the right approach and support, it is possible to recover and regain control of your life. One approach to overcoming drug addiction is a gradual tapering down method, where the amount of the drug consumed is gradually reduced over time to avoid severe withdrawal symptoms and reduce the risk of relapse.

The following de-addiction plan is designed to help individuals gradually taper down and ultimately eliminate their addiction. This plan is a general framework and can be tailored to fit various types of addictions, including drug addiction, alcohol addiction, gambling addiction, pornography addiction, and other forms of addictive behavior. It's important to note that this plan is not a substitute for professional medical or psychological treatment and is best implemented under the guidance of a healthcare professional.

Week 1: During the first week, maintain your current level of consumption, but begin to track your behavior and triggers that lead to your addiction. Use this time to reflect on your goals and prepare yourself for the tapering process.

Week 2-3: In these two weeks, reduce your consumption by 30%. For example, if you were drinking three alcoholic beverages per day, reduce to two per day for two weeks. Use the same reduction percentage for other forms of addiction.

Week 4: In this week, reduce your consumption by another 30%. For example, if you were drinking two alcoholic beverages per day, reduce to one per day for one week.

Week 5: In this week, reduce your consumption to every other day. For example, if you were drinking one alcoholic beverage per day, reduce to one alcoholic beverage every other day.

Week 6: In this week, increase the gap between consumption to two days. For example, if you were drinking one alcoholic beverage every other day, reduce to one alcoholic beverage every two days.

Week 7: In this week, increase the gap to three days. For example, if you were drinking one alcoholic beverage every two days, reduce to one alcoholic beverage every three days.

Week 8: In this final week, reduce your consumption to half and maintain a gap of three days between consumption. For example, if you were drinking one alcoholic beverage every three days, reduce to half of one alcoholic beverage every three days. Continue to reduce until you have eliminated the addiction completely by the end of the week.

Conclusion: This 8-week de-addiction plan provides a general framework that can be used to taper down various types of addictions. It's important to approach this process with patience, perseverance, and the guidance of a healthcare professional. While this plan can be helpful in reducing and eliminating addiction, it's important to seek additional support and resources as needed to maintain sobriety and prevent relapse.

De-addiction plan #2

Dealing with addiction can be a difficult journey, but it is not an impossible one. With the right mindset and a well-structured plan, it is possible to overcome addiction and regain control of your life. This 8-week universal de-addiction plan is designed to help you taper off from any type of substance or behavior addiction gradually, with a focus on self-management.

Week 1: Preparation and goal-setting. The first week is all about getting mentally prepared for the journey ahead. Identify the addiction that you want to quit and set a specific goal for the end of the 8-week period. Write down your reasons for wanting to quit, and create a plan for achieving your goal.

Week 2: Self-awareness and coping strategies. This week, focus on becoming more aware of your triggers and developing coping strategies to deal with them. Take note of situations or emotions that make you want to turn to your addiction and develop alternative ways of coping with them.

Week 3: Creating a support network. It's important to have people in your life who support your decision to quit your addiction. Use this week to reach out to friends or family members who can provide emotional support and encouragement. You can also consider joining support groups or seeking professional counseling.

Week 4: Developing healthy habits. This week, focus on developing healthy habits to replace your addiction. Consider taking up exercise, meditation, or other activities that you enjoy and that can help improve your overall well-being.

Week 5: Reducing consumption. It's time to start tapering off your addiction. Use this week to reduce your consumption by 30%

and keep a log of your progress.

Week 6: Continued reduction. This week, continue to reduce your consumption by 30%. If you find it difficult, remind yourself of your reasons for quitting and the progress you've already made.

Week 7: Further reduction. Reduce your consumption by 30% again, and focus on staying motivated and committed to your goal.

Week 8: Final stretch. This is the final week of the program. Reduce your consumption to every three days, and by the end of the week, stop consumption completely. Celebrate your accomplishment and continue to focus on healthy habits and coping strategies to maintain your sobriety.

Remember that overcoming addiction is a journey, and it's important to be kind to yourself along the way. With a strong support network, self-awareness, healthy habits, and a commitment to your goal, you can successfully overcome addiction and take control of your life.

CHAPTER EIGHTEEN

Positive Self-affirmations

Positive affirmations are statements that reflect positive thoughts, beliefs, and feelings. Practicing positive affirmations can help shift your mindset and promote self-compassion, confidence, and resilience. To practice positive affirmations, find a quiet and comfortable space, take a few deep breaths, and repeat the affirmation to yourself, either out loud or silently. You can also write down your affirmations or create visual reminders, such as sticky notes or posters, to help reinforce positive self-programming throughout the day. Making positive affirmations a daily practice can be a powerful tool for healing from mental health disorders. Start by selecting affirmations that resonate with you, and try repeating them to yourself each day. This could be done during your morning routine, while commuting, or at bedtime. It may also be helpful to write your affirmations down or display them in a place where you can see them frequently, such as on your bathroom mirror or computer desktop. Remember to practice your affirmations with intention and try to believe in the truth behind them. If you find it difficult to believe in your affirmations at first, start with small, achievable statements and work your way up. With regular practice, positive affirmations can help shift your mindset and promote self-compassion, confidence, and resilience, ultimately helping you develop immunity for mental health.

Customizing your affirmations can also help increase their effectiveness in supporting your mental health. While the affirmations listed above can be a good starting point, it's important to choose statements that resonate with you personally. If you have trouble believing in an affirmation or it doesn't feel genuine, try rephrasing it in a way that does. For example, if the affirmation "I am worthy of love and respect" feels too general or overwhelming, you could try breaking it down into smaller statements that feel more achievable, such as "I am taking steps to practice self-care and prioritize my needs" or "I am deserving of kindness and compassion from myself and others." Additionally, consider incorporating specifics into your affirmations. If you're struggling with anxiety related to public speaking, for instance, try an affirmation like "I am confident and capable of delivering a strong presentation" rather than a more general affirmation like "I am calm and centered." By tailoring your affirmations to your unique needs and circumstances, you can make them more effective tools for promoting mental well-being.

Depression:

- I am capable of healing and recovery.
- I am strong and resilient.
- I am deserving of love and happiness.
- I am taking steps to improve my mental health.
- I am surrounded by people who love and support me.
- I am more than my thoughts and feelings.
- I am worthy of self-care and self-compassion.
- I am grateful for the blessings in my life.
- I am open to new opportunities and experiences.
- I am embracing my strengths and abilities.
- I am moving forward and creating a better future for myself.
- I am learning and growing every day.

Anxiety:

- I am calm and at ease.

- I am in control of my thoughts and feelings.
- I am capable of managing my anxiety.
- I am more than my anxiety.
- I am taking steps to manage my anxiety.
- I am learning new coping strategies every day.
- I am surrounded by love and support.
- I am grateful for the blessings in my life.
- I am capable of finding joy and pleasure in my life.
- I am embracing uncertainty and change.
- I am creating a better future for myself through self-care and self-love.
- I am capable of achieving my goals.

Post-Traumatic Stress Disorder (PTSD):

- I am worthy of healing and recovery.
- I am safe and protected.
- I am capable of finding peace and calm.
- I am learning to process my trauma in healthy ways.
- I am making progress in my healing journey.
- I am stronger than my trauma.
- I am more than my trauma.
- I am capable of finding joy and happiness in my life.
- I am embracing my strengths and abilities.
- I am taking care of myself and my needs.
- I am worthy of love and compassion.
- I am capable of overcoming my fears and doubts.

Bipolar Disorder:

- I am capable of finding stability and balance.

- I am taking care of myself and my needs.
- I am learning to manage my moods in healthy ways.
- I am more than my diagnosis.
- I am surrounded by love and support.
- I am worthy of self-care and self-compassion.
- I am taking steps to improve my mental health.
- I am grateful for the blessings in my life.
- I am open to new opportunities and experiences.
- I am embracing my strengths and abilities.
- I am creating a better future for myself.
- I am capable of managing my bipolar disorder.

Obsessive-Compulsive Disorder (OCD):

- I am more than my thoughts and compulsions.
- I am capable of finding peace and calm.
- I am taking steps to manage my OCD.
- I am worthy of love and compassion.
- I am learning new coping strategies every day.
- I am grateful for the blessings in my life.
- I am stronger than my OCD.
- I am embracing my strengths and abilities.
- I am worthy of self-care and self-compassion.
- I am capable of managing my OCD.
- I am creating a better future for myself.
- I am moving forward and achieving my goals.

Eating Disorders:

- I am worthy of love and acceptance.
- I am capable of healing and recovery.

- I am taking care of my body and my needs.
- I am more than my appearance.
- I am embracing my strengths and abilities.
- I am grateful for the blessings in my life.
- I am learning to nourish my body and mind.
- I am capable of finding balance and harmony.
- I am worthy of self-care and self-compassion.
- I am creating a better future for myself.
- I am stronger than my eating disorder.
- I am capable of achieving my goals.

Substance Abuse:

- I am worthy of healing and recovery.
- I am capable of overcoming addiction.
- I am taking steps to manage my substance abuse.
- I am surrounded by love and support.
- I am more than my addiction.
- I am learning new coping strategies every day.
- I am grateful for the blessings in my life.
- I am capable of finding joy and happiness in sobriety.
- I am embracing my strengths and abilities.
- I am taking care of myself and my needs.
- I am creating a better future for myself.
- I am capable of achieving my goals.

Borderline Personality Disorder:

- I am worthy of love and acceptance.
- I am capable of healing and recovery.
- I am learning to manage my emotions in healthy ways.

- I am more than my diagnosis.
- I am taking steps to improve my mental health.
- I am surrounded by love and support.
- I am grateful for the blessings in my life.
- I am embracing my strengths and abilities.
- I am worthy of self-care and self-compassion.
- I am creating a better future for myself.
- I am stronger than my challenges.
- I am capable of finding stability and balance.

CHAPTER NINETEEN

Diet & Nutrition

Food plays a crucial role in our mental health. A balanced diet, rich in vitamins, minerals, and nutrients, can help support brain function, improve mood, and reduce the risk of mental health disorders. In India, we have a rich culinary tradition, and there are many local foods that can help promote mental well-being.

Here's a guide to some of the best foods for improving mental health, and how to incorporate them into your diet.

1. Whole Grains: Whole grains, such as brown rice, quinoa, and millets, are rich in complex carbohydrates that can help regulate blood sugar levels and improve mood. They also contain B vitamins, which are important for brain function and may help reduce the risk of depression. Whole grains are a staple in many Indian diets, so incorporating them into your meals is easy. Try swapping out white rice for brown rice, or incorporating millets like jowar or bajra into your roti or dosa batter.
2. Leafy Greens: Leafy greens, such as spinach, kale, and methi, are packed with vitamins and minerals that are essential for brain health. They are particularly rich in folate, a B vitamin that is important for the production of serotonin, a neurotransmitter that regulates mood. Leafy greens are also a good source of magnesium, which can help reduce anxiety and promote relaxation. Try incorporating leafy greens into your diet by adding them to your curries, smoothies, or salads.

3. Nuts and Seeds: Nuts and seeds, such as almonds, walnuts, pumpkin seeds, and flaxseeds, are rich in omega-3 fatty acids, which are essential for brain function and can help reduce inflammation. They also contain magnesium, which can help reduce anxiety, and zinc, which is important for regulating mood. Nuts and seeds can be a healthy snack or added to meals, such as in chutneys, salads, or smoothies.
4. Fermented Foods : Fermented foods, such as yogurt, kefir, and pickles, are rich in probiotics, which can improve gut health and promote the production of neurotransmitters like serotonin. Gut health has been linked to mental health, and a healthy gut can help reduce anxiety and depression. Fermented foods are a staple in many Indian diets, so incorporating them into your meals is easy. Try adding a dollop of yogurt to your curry, or munching on pickles as a side dish.
5. Spices and Herbs : Spices and herbs, such as turmeric, cumin, coriander, and ginger, are used extensively in Indian cuisine and have been shown to have many health benefits. Turmeric, in particular, has anti-inflammatory properties that can help reduce the risk of depression and other mental health disorders. Spices and herbs can be added to almost any dish, and can also be brewed as teas or added to smoothies for an extra boost of nutrition.
6. Legumes : Legumes, such as lentils, chickpeas, and kidney beans, are an important source of protein in many Indian diets. They are also a good source of complex carbohydrates, which can help regulate blood sugar levels and improve mood. Legumes are also rich in folate, which is important for brain function, and iron, which is important for energy and mood. Try incorporating legumes into your meals by adding them to your curries or salads.
7. Fruits : Fruits are packed with essential vitamins, minerals, and antioxidants that can benefit mental health. For example, berries are high in antioxidants and have been linked to improved cognitive function and reduced risk of depression. Oranges are

a good source of vitamin C, which can reduce inflammation and boost the immune system. Bananas are high in potassium, which can help regulate blood pressure and reduce stress. Other fruits like apples, pomegranates, and grapes have also been shown to have positive effects on mental health. Incorporating a variety of fruits into your diet can help provide the nutrients needed to support optimal brain function and reduce the risk of mental health disorders.

8. Ayurvedic herbs : In addition to the above-mentioned foods, there are many Ayurvedic herbs that are believed to have positive effects on mental health. Ashwagandha is a popular adaptogen herb that has been shown to reduce stress and anxiety, improve cognitive function, and regulate hormones. Brahmi is another herb that is used to enhance memory and improve cognitive function. Tulsi, or holy basil, is a powerful antioxidant that can help reduce inflammation and improve overall health. These herbs can be consumed as supplements or added to teas and other recipes.
9. Water : Drinking enough water is important for overall health, including mental health. Dehydration can lead to headaches, fatigue, and other symptoms that can impact mood and cognitive function. Aim to drink at least 8-10 glasses of water per day, and more if you are active or live in a hot climate. You can also drink coconut water or herbal teas to stay hydrated. If you use RO-purified water, it is recommended to consume one sachet of ORS/electoral daily.

What you eat can have a significant impact on your mood, energy levels, and overall mental well-being. In this guide, we will now explore 10 things to avoid in your diet in order to promote optimal mental health. By avoiding these following foods and ingredients, you can help to reduce inflammation, balance blood sugar levels, and support the health of your brain and body.

1. Sugar and refined carbohydrates: Foods high in sugar and refined carbohydrates can cause blood sugar levels to spike and then crash, which can lead to mood swings, fatigue, and anxiety. Additionally, consuming these foods regularly can increase the risk of inflammation and other health issues that can negatively impact mental health.
2. Artificial sweeteners: While artificial sweeteners may seem like a healthier alternative to sugar, they can actually have negative effects on mental health. Some studies suggest that consuming artificial sweeteners can increase the risk of depression, anxiety, and other mental health disorders.
3. Processed and packaged foods: Processed and packaged foods are often high in unhealthy fats, salt, and other additives that can negatively impact mental health. Eating a diet high in these foods can lead to inflammation, hormone imbalances, and other health issues that can increase the risk of mental health disorders.
4. Trans fats: Trans fats are a type of unhealthy fat that are often found in processed and fried foods. Consuming these fats on a regular basis can lead to inflammation, insulin resistance, and other health issues that can increase the risk of mental health disorders.
5. Alcohol: While moderate alcohol consumption has been linked to some health benefits, excessive alcohol consumption can have negative effects on mental health. Alcohol can disrupt sleep patterns, lead to anxiety and depression, and even increase the risk of suicide.
6. High-sodium foods: Foods high in sodium, such as processed meats, canned foods, and some snack foods, can lead to increased blood pressure and other health issues that can negatively impact mental health. Additionally, consuming too much salt can disrupt the balance of important minerals in the body.
7. Fried and greasy foods: Fried and greasy foods can lead to inflammation and other health issues that can negatively impact

mental health. Consuming these foods on a regular basis can increase the risk of mental health disorders and other health issues.

8. Fast food: Fast food is often high in unhealthy fats, salt, and calories, and low in nutrients. Consuming fast food regularly can lead to weight gain, inflammation, and other health issues that can negatively impact mental health.
9. Foods high in saturated fats: Foods high in saturated fats, such as red meat and full-fat dairy products, can lead to inflammation and other health issues that can negatively impact mental health. Consuming these foods on a regular basis can increase the risk of mental health disorders and other health issues.
10. Processed snack foods: Processed snack foods, such as chips, cookies, and candy, are often high in sugar, refined carbohydrates, and unhealthy fats. Consuming these foods regularly can lead to blood sugar imbalances, inflammation, and other health issues that can negatively impact mental health.

CHAPTER TWENTY

EMDR Self-Therapy

EMDR therapy (Eye Movement Desensitization and Reprocessing) is a unique and highly effective approach to psychotherapy that has been used for over 30 years to help individuals process and overcome negative thoughts, emotions, and experiences. It has been recognized as a proven treatment for a wide range of mental health issues, including anxiety disorders, depression disorders, and trauma and stress-related disorders. Unlike other forms of therapy, EMDR therapy involves the use of eye movements, tapping, or other forms of bilateral stimulation to stimulate the brain's natural ability to process and integrate difficult experiences. By activating both sides of the brain through these simple techniques, EMDR therapy can help individuals work through traumatic memories and experiences in a safe and controlled way, without becoming overwhelmed or retraumatized.

While it is typically done with the guidance of a trained therapist, there are some steps you can take to practice EMDR therapy on your own. By following these steps, you can potentially find relief from negative beliefs and experiences that are holding you back in your life. Whether you are dealing with anxiety, depression, or the aftermath of a traumatic event, EMDR therapy can help you move past your challenges and live a more fulfilling and satisfying life.

1. Choose a focus: Choose a negative belief or situation that causes you to feel anxious.

2. Rate your level of distress: On a scale of 0-10, rate the level of distress caused by the focus you have chosen.
3. Begin the eye movement: Sit comfortably and focus on the negative belief or situation that causes you anxiety. Next, look to your left side as far as you can see while still keeping your head straight. Then, look to your right side as far as you can see while still keeping your head straight.
4. Focus on the issue: While looking to your left and right side, focus on the negative belief or situation that causes you anxiety, that causes you to feel depressed, or any traumatic memory/ experience about which you overthink.
5. Continue the eye movement: Keep looking to your left and right side for a few minutes or until you feel a sense of calm and relief.
6. Rate your level of distress again: After the eye movement, rate your level of distress again on a scale of 0-10. You may find that your distress has decreased or that your perception of the issue has changed.

It's important to note that while this technique can be helpful, it's always best to work with a therapist for complex issues.

Conclusion

As we come to the end of this book, I hope that the information and techniques you have learned will help you build a strong and resilient immune system for your mind. Remember, just as your body can be strengthened and protected against physical illnesses, your mind can also be strengthened and protected against mental health challenges. It is important to understand that while the techniques outlined in this book can be incredibly helpful, they are not a substitute for professional help. If you are struggling with a mental health issue, it is important to seek the help of a qualified professional.

As a practicing psychologist and psychotherapist, I have helped thousands of people overcome a wide variety of mental health challenges. I have seen the profound impact that personalized treatment can have on a person's life, and I am dedicated to providing that level of care to each and every one of my patients. If you have read this book and feel that you could benefit from more personalized treatment, please do not hesitate to reach out to me. My goal is to help you achieve long-term success and wellbeing, not just temporary relief from symptoms. Together, we can work to uncover the root causes of your mental health challenges and develop a personalized treatment plan that works for you.

I want to thank you for taking the time to read this book and for your commitment to your own mental health. Remember that building a strong immune system for your mind is an ongoing process that requires commitment and dedication. But with the right tools and support, you can overcome any mental health challenge and achieve a happier, more fulfilling life.

As a psychologist and psychotherapist, I am committed to providing personalized and effective treatments to individuals struggling with mental health issues. My clinical experience has shown that many individuals are not able to receive the care they need due to various reasons such as financial constraints, social stigma, or lack of access to mental health services. Through this book, I aim to provide accessible and effective coping mechanisms that can be used to manage and heal a wide variety of mental health problems. However, I also understand that every individual's experiences and needs are unique, and no one coping mechanism or treatment plan can work for everyone. That's why I encourage you to reach out to me directly for personalized treatment that takes into account your unique situation and needs. Whether you are dealing with anxiety, depression, trauma, or any other mental health issue, I am here to help.

My approach to treatment is grounded in evidence-based techniques and is tailored to the individual's needs. I believe in a holistic approach that takes into account the biological, psychological, and social factors that contribute to mental health problems. My goal is not just to alleviate symptoms, but to help individuals achieve long-term mental wellness and thrive in their personal and professional lives. I understand that seeking help for mental health issues can be a difficult and vulnerable experience. That's why I strive to provide a safe and supportive environment where individuals can feel heard, understood, and empowered to take charge of their mental health.

If you are ready to take the next step towards healing and improving your mental well-being, please do not hesitate to reach out to me. You can find my contact information below. Remember, your mental health matters, and seeking help is a sign of strength, not weakness. I am here to help, and I look forward to working with you on your journey towards mental wellness.

Author's contact details :

- Email : contact.nitnem@gmail.com
- Mobile : +91 9235344444 (whatsapp texts only)

Congratulations on taking the first step towards mental wellness by reading this book! Remember, taking care of your mental health is a lifelong journey, and the coping mechanisms and guidance provided in this book are meant to be used as a tool in your arsenal. Use it as a guide and practice the techniques consistently to strengthen your mental immune system Remember, you are not alone in this journey, and I am always here to support you in any way I can. Keep working towards your mental health, and the rewards will be worth it. As you close the final pages of this book, remember that taking care of your mental health is a lifelong journey. It's not a one-time fix, but rather a continuous effort that requires daily attention and nurturing. Just as we maintain our physical health through exercise, healthy eating, and rest, we must also prioritize our mental well-being. It's important to remember that setbacks may occur, but they don't define you. Don't be discouraged by bumps in the road, instead, use them as opportunities to learn, grow, and become more resilient. By taking care of your mental health, you are not only helping yourself, but also those around you. So, keep working towards a healthy mind, and don't hesitate to reach out for support when you need it.

Printed by Libri Plureos GmbH in Hamburg,
Germany